The Art
of
Painting
on
Silk

Volume 4
Potpourri

The Art of Painting on Silk

Volume 4
Potpourri

Edited by Pam Dawson
Translated by Kate Horgan

Search Press

First published in Great Britain 1990
Search Press Ltd
Wellwood, North Farm Road, Tunbridge Wells, Kent TN2 3DR

This book has been rewritten and rearranged from original French editions of *Peinture sur Soie* copyright © Les Editions de Saxe-Peinture sur Soie 1985, 1986, 1987, 1988

English version *The Art of Painting on Silk Volume 4-Potpourri* Copyright © Search Press Limited 1990

The designs shown in this book are created by the following artists: pages 7, 39, 40, 41, 42, 43, 49, 64, 65, 67, 69, 71 Akane Kinu; pages 9, 12, 15, 16, 17, 21, 25, 27, 34, 36, 37, 46, 47, 50, 53, 56, 59, 60, 61, 62, 63, 75, 79, 80, 81 Joelle Dreville; page 78 Mauricette Feuillade; pages 19, 73 Annick Blanck; page 22 Sylvie Leveque; page 77 Michele Vinial; pages 31, 33 Renée Costes.

Translated by Kate Horgan

ISBN 0 85532 646 8

Converting centimetres to inches

centimetres	inches
1.25	½
2	¾
2.5	1
3	1¼
3.5	1⅜
4	1½
4.5	1¾
5	2
5.5	2⅛
6	2¼
6.5	2½
7	2¾
7.5	3
8	3¼
8.5	3⅜
9	3½
10	4
20	7¾
30	11¾
40	15¾
50	19¾
60	23½
70	27½
80	31½
90	35½
100	39½

Phototypeset by Scribe Design, 123 Watling Street, Gillingham, Kent
Printed and bound in Spain by Salingraf S.A.L. Bilbao

CONTENTS

Introduction

Silk is one of the most luxurious materials known to mankind and its history stretches back into the mists of time. The finished fabric has a sheen and glow quite unlike that of any other fibre and when completed with an original hand-painted design, the result is unique.

Silk production, or sericulture, is an agricultural process during which vegetation is converted into protein by an animal – the silkworm! The caterpillar of the Bombyx Mori moth feeds solely on leaves, mainly from the mulberry tree, extruding them as a viscous protein solution which forms the basis of silk thread. The filament is produced by a pair of glands running the length of the worm's body and is extruded through an opening in the top of its head. The filaments from each gland remain separate but are bonded together by a protein called 'Sericin'. To produce 0.5 kg/1 lb of raw silk, the worm must consume about 101.06 kilo/2 cwt of foliage. As it prepares to emerge as a moth, the caterpillar spins this continuous fine thread round its body to protect itself.

Silk originally came from China via a trade route stretching some 11,265 km/7,000 m and the penalty for smuggling silkworms out of the country was death. As a result, only the finished fabric reached the outside world but, in the sixth century, monks are believed to have hidden the eggs of the silkworm in their staffs and smuggled them into Byzantium. Both the Greeks and Romans referred to China as 'Seres', and it is from this name that the word 'silk' is derived.

China's main export along this route was silk but it was not until the nineteenth century that the German geographer, Ferdinand von Richthofen, first used the word, 'Seidenstrasse' or 'Silk Road' to describe this caravan trail, which had been known for centuries. In the west, the silk road began on the Mediterranean coast, in such ports as Antioch and Alexandria, working its way through Mesopotamia and Western Turkestan and eventually reached Ch'ang-an in China – the city known today as Xi'an.

The Worshiptul Company of Weavers was founded in Spitalfields in 1155 but, at that time, only a few members would have been involved in silk weaving, mainly ribbons and laces. The growth of the Italian City States, such as Florence and Venice, due to their flourishing silk industries, prompted James I of England to invite French silk weavers to settle in the country in the early seventeenth century. The industry progressed and prospered until 1674, when large imports of French silk caused a slump in trade. The failure of the industry to cut costs by the introduction of new production techniques was a factor in its eventual decline in this country.

Due to present-day production methods and the extensive cultivation of silk worms, silk is available in almost every country in the world and is becoming popular as a fashion and furnishing fabric. Although these materials may appear to be delicate, they will stand up extremely well to normal wear and tear, although not to excessively rough handling – painted silk should be washed by hand.

Two attributes are essential for the silk artist; not necessarily drawing skill and colour sense, as might be expected, but patience and diligence. With these two qualities the basic skills of painting on silk can be explored and mastered and, nowadays, even a complete beginner can achieve excellent results with modern silk paints.

Although silk painting is not an exorbitantly expensive hobby it is certainly not cheap as silk is still a precious material. Nor can it be guaranteed that your first attempt will be a masterpiece! If you are a novice in both painting and dressmaking, it is best to start with a small-scale design on a remnant of silk, which can be used as a decorative handkerchief or a personal greetings card. This book is full of simple and more complex designs, explaining the techniques used in the craft and giving advice on how to overcome some of the errors you may experience with your first efforts.

Once you begin to experiment, however, you will soon discover what a wealth of possibilities the craft has to offer, for no other method of painting can produce such luminous colours or magical results.

Opposite: winter, from a set of cushions and wall hangings depicting the four seasons. See pages 41 and 45 for instructions and charts.

Greetings cards and wall hangings

Your friends will be delighted to receive a hand-painted card to mark a special anniversary and these small projects will enable you to experiment with the various silk painting techniques.

Your next step could be the ideal gift of a hand-painted wall hanging. This can be mounted in a similar way to a greetings card, or backed with lining fabric and completed with wooden dowelling at the top and lower edges.

The details given in this section will enable you to mount your own cards and complete a wall hanging with the minimum of expense.

Mounting a greetings card

A wide selection of pre-cut mounts is available, complete with matching envelopes, and these will give your silk painting a professional finish. It is a simple matter, however, to make your own mounts to any size and the card or paper you use will vary in price according to quality and weight. Choose the colour of your mount very carefully, making sure it will enhance your silk painting. A pad of assorted coloured cartridge paper offers a wide variety of choice. Before finally deciding on the size and colour of your mount, make sure you can obtain an envelope to match!

Cutting the mount

In addition to the mounting card you will also need sharp scissors, a ruler for trimming the card to size and some glue. Rubber solution is recommended, as it allows the picture to be repositioned if necessary.

For a greetings card, cut a rectangle and fold this in half, making sure that this size will accommodate the silk painting. On the left-hand side, which will be the inside of the front of the card, mark an area large enough to allow a full view of the painting, allowing about 1 cm/½ in of the picture to be stuck down all round, and leaving a margin of at least 2.5 cm/1 in all round the edges of the card. Cut out this marked section, (Fig a).

With the right side of the silk painting facing you, lightly apply the glue to the extreme edges, as directed. Place the painting face down on to the inside of the cut-out opening, making sure it is correctly positioned.

Once the glue is dry, fold the card in half so that the painting shows on the front and write your message on the inside.

For a larger silk painting which is to be mounted on card and displayed as a wall hanging, cut a piece of card large enough to take the silk painting and allowing a margin of at least 2.5 cm/1 in all

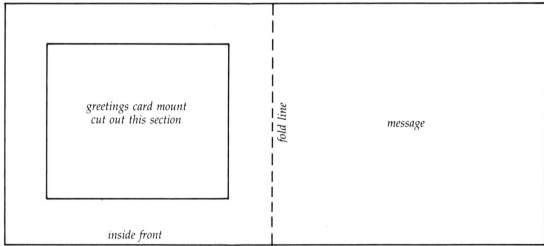

greetings card mount
cut out this section

fold line

message

inside front

fig a

Opposite: use this decorative alphabet as a colourful 'sampler' of your skill, or simply use the letters to add your initials to a design. See page 23 for the instructions and chart.

round the edges of the card. Mark and cut the viewing area, and stick the painting down as given for a greetings card. Once the glue is dry, cut another piece of card to the same size as the first piece and stick down the ends of a length of cord so that the painting can be hung up. Stick this card to the back of the original card, sandwiching the cord between the two pieces.

Framing a wall hanging

Choose a subject for your wall hanging which will add to the atmosphere of the room; strong and bold for a living area but soft and subtle for a bedroom. Use colours which will complement the decor of the room and choose a position which will allow the wall hanging to be a focal point in the room without being subjected to too much direct sunlight, as this will gradually fade the colours.

Assembling the frame

In addition to the completed silk painting, already fixed and pressed as directed by the paint manufacturers, you will require white cotton backing material, the same size as the picture. You will also need four lengths of semi-circular wooden dowelling, 2.5 cm/1 in in diameter, to the width of the hanging and allowing about 2 cm/ ¾ in extra at each end, plus a tube of glue and cord for hanging.

If you wish to paint or stain the wooden dowelling in a colour that will harmonise with your design, this must be done and the wood allowed to dry thoroughly, before sticking it in place.

Place the silk painting and the white backing material together, with the right sides facing each other. Tack, or pin along the two side edges, leaving the top and lower edges open, then seam these edges. Turn to the right side and press lightly on the backing fabric.

fig b *completing the lower edge of a wall hanging*

Glue the first length of dowelling to the wrong side of the lower edge of the hanging, then glue the raw edges of both pieces of fabric to the dowelling. Carefully place the second piece of dowelling on top of the first piece, concealing the raw edges of the fabric and glue in place, (Fig b). Finish the top edge in the same way, placing the ends of the length of cord between the two pieces of dowelling before glueing in place, (Fig c).

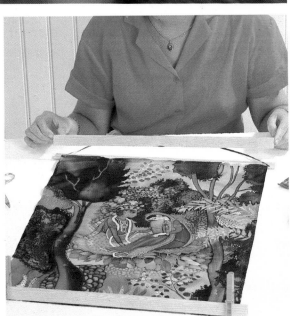

fig c *completing the top edge of a wall hanging*

Flower panel for box or card

This panel measures 12 cm/4¾ in wide by 17 cm/6¾ in long but can be enlarged or reduced to suit your own requirements.

Materials

Fabric: silk pongé 5, 14 cm/5½ in wide by 19 cm/7½ in long.

Paints: ruby red, bright pink, burgundy, yellow gold, brown, lime green, jade, black and combinations of these colours as well as diluted versions.

Gutta: colourless.

Method examples

Sprinkle the damp petals with fine salt and use rough salt for the background.

To mount the silk on a box lid, first stick it to a piece of thin card, then use double-sided tape to fix it in position. Neaten the edges with a toning, non-fray ribbon, mitred at the corners.

enlarge or reduce to suit your own requirements

Opposite: *a selection of simple designs to use as greetings cards or small wall hangings. See pages 14 to 15 for instructions and charts.*

Scenic wall hanging

This wall hanging measures 20 cm/ 7¾ in wide by 17 cm/6¾ in deep but can be enlarged or reduced to suit your own requirements.

Materials
Fabric: silk pongé 5, 22 cm/8¾ in wide by 20 cm/7¾ in deep.

Paints: azure blue, duck egg blue, jade, poppy red, cornflower blue, yellow gold, old gold, brown and combinations of these colours as well as diluted versions.

Gutta: colourless.

Method examples
Apply the colour in patches, while the background fields are still damp.

enlarge or reduce to suit your own requirements

Panel for box or card

This panel measures 16 cm/6¼ in wide by 12 cm/4¾ in deep but can be enlarged or reduced to suit your own requirements.

Materials

Fabric: silk pongé 5, 19 cm/7½ in wide by 14 cm/5½ in deep.

Paints: bright pink, azure blue, duck egg blue, cornflower blue, jade, black and combinations of these colours as well as diluted versions.

Gutta: black for the train, white for the mountains.

Method examples

While the foreground surface and the mountains are still damp, sprinkle with fine salt and apply the colour in patches.

1.5 cm

Snow scenes

These two cards are inspired by scenes of Japanese landscapes. They measure 12 cm/4¾ in wide by 15.5 cm/6 in deep.

Materials

Fabric: silk pongé 5, 14 cm/5½ in wide by 18 cm/7 in deep.

Paints: chrome yellow, azure blue, navy blue, black, lime green and combinations of these colours as well as diluted versions, also white fabric paint.

Gutta: black.

Method examples

It is important to shade well. Shade between the water and sky from black to grey, through navy and azure blue, leaving a narrow colourless band.

Use very little colour for the ground and trees. When it is all completely dry, dot with small dabs of white paint to represent the snow.

1.5 cm

1.5 cm

Magnolias by moonlight wall hanging

This wall hanging measures 38 cm/ 15 in wide by 52 cm/20½ in long when finished.

Materials

Fabric: silk pongé 5, 41 cm/16¼ in wide by 55 cm/21¾ in long.

Paints: pink, yellow gold, amethyst, lime green, black, azure blue, duck egg blue, brown, tobacco brown and combinations of these colours as well as diluted versions.

Gutta: pink for the blossoms, black for the trees and branches.

Method examples

The flowers should be very pale. The pink is slightly tinted with amethyst and diluted. Once the flowers are painted, apply antifusant to the entire surface and paint the different planes in succession, allowing each to dry before going on to the next one.

Use the browns and a little lime green for the branches, shade well and add a few drops of alcohol to the surface when dry.

Sprinkle rough salt on to the grey and duck egg blue foreground. When completely dry, paint the small plants and leaves in black and brown.

6 cm

Birds of spring pictures

Only one drawing is used, split into two parts which can be separate, placed together or juxtaposed, depending on the arrangement you prefer. The finished paintings can be mounted on card, as shown, or framed. Each one measures 30 cm/11¾ in wide by 46 cm/18 in long.

Materials

Fabric: silk pongé 7, 33 cm/13 in wide by 50 cm/19¾ in long for each card.

Paints: caramel, azure blue, sun yellow and combinations of these colours as well as diluted versions.

Gutta: strong beige, brown felt pen or caramel tinted thickener applied with a drawing pen.

Method examples

The background is painted with very diluted caramel. The branches and leaves are mid-to-strong caramel, alternating with a little azure blue added to the clear zones. Leave to dry and then push the colour to the edges of the gutta with a mixture of water and alcohol. Repeat until you achieve the effect you desire.

The flowers are only coloured in the centre – this why the gutta must be strongly tinted – with a dot of azure blue and a small circle painted freehand, shaded slightly with very diluted caramel. Finally, mark in the stamens in little dots with a felt pen or caramel coloured thickener.

Shade the breast and wings of the birds very lightly with sun yellow, using a fine paintbrush dipped in a little paint. Then redraw the feathers freehand, within the gutta limits, in mid and strong caramel.

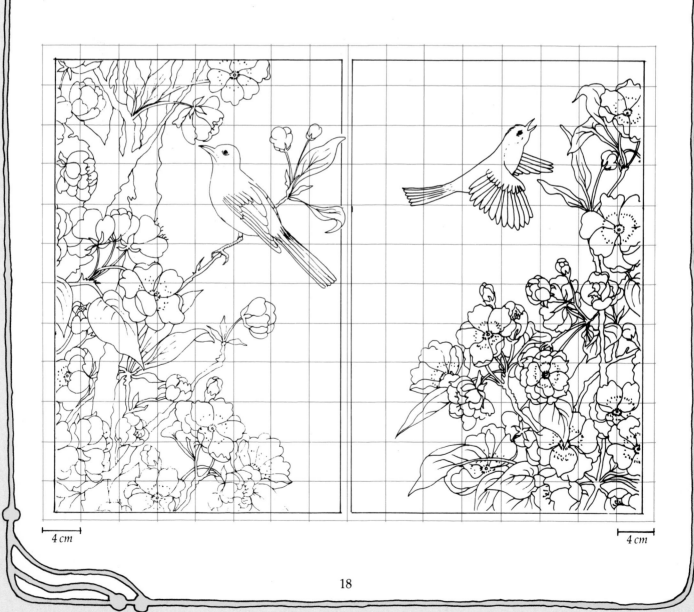

4 cm

4 cm

18

Landscape wall hanging

This wall hanging measures 38 cm/ 15 in wide by 52 cm/20½ in long.

Materials

Fabric: silk pongé 5, 42 cm/16½ in wide by 56 cm/22 in long.

Paints: navy blue, vermilion red, azure blue, yellow, old gold, lime green, green, beige, ochre and combinations of these colours as well as diluted versions.

Gutta: grey, and a little black printing ink.

Method examples

This painting is very detailed and will require great patience when applying the gutta.

The mound in the foreground is spotted with alcohol.

3 cm

Sunset picture

This naive painting measures 24 cm/9½ in wide by 18 cm/7 in deep. The edges have been deliberately frayed before mounting the picture on card. If you wish to conceal the edges, allow about 2 cm/¾ in extra all round.

Materials

Fabric: silk pongé 5 or 9, 24 cm/9½ in in wide by 18 cm/7 in deep, or as required.

Paints: yellow, fuchsia, violet, turquoise, green, brown and combinations of these colours as well as diluted versions.

Method examples

You do not need any hard-or-fast gutta lines when painting a naive picture. Fill in the pastel background first, then using a No 20 paintbrush, trace diluted yellow, pink and violet lines, then work over the background to blur the separations.

While the paint is still damp, colour the hills in diluted brown. Apply anti-fusant and leave to dry.

Use a No 4 paintbrush for the houses and with No 2 and 0 paintbrushes, add details of the trees with a little pure colour.

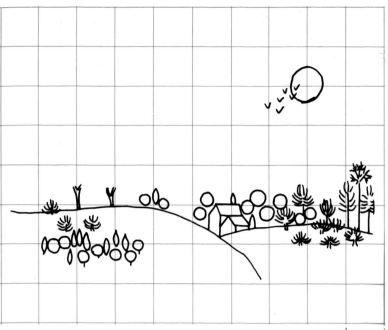

2.5 cm

Alphabet panel

This panel measures 56 cm/22 in wide and 75 cm/29½ in long when finished.

Materials

Fabric: silk pongé 7, 60 cm/23½ in wide by 79 cm/31 in long.

Paints: poppy red, pink, fuchsia, jade, yellow gold, azure blue, amethyst, tobacco brown and combinations of these colours as well as diluted versions.

Gutta: green, black, yellow, pink and blue.

Method examples

Match the colour of the gutta to the shape to be outlined. Use black gutta for dark hair and eyes.

Use pale pink with a dot of tobacco brown to colour the bodies and faces. Add a brighter spot to the faces while still damp. Shade the flowers and leaves with very diluted colours.

Paint one wide band and three narrow ones for the border, in whatever colours you prefer.

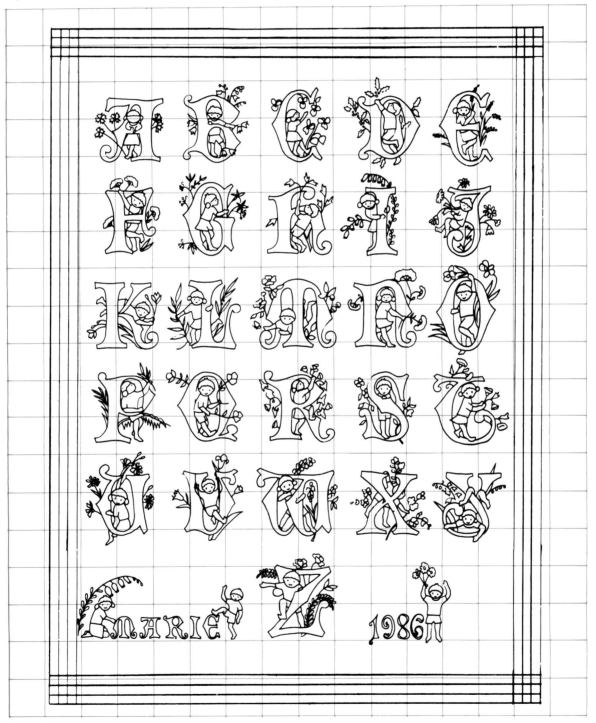

4 cm

Shawls and scarves

A hand-painted silk shawl or scarf is a luxurious and fashionable accessory and deserves to be finished in the best possible way. Many of the designs featured in this book automatically have their edges concealed by various sewing or framing methods, but this is not possible when completing a scarf or handkerchief, as the edges remain visible.

A shawl that is to be completed with a fringe can be finished with straight machine hemming, as the edges will be hidden by the braid on the fringing. Alternatively, you may prefer to leave the edges of a square unseamed, to give a soft, frayed effect.

To give a perfect finish to a scarf or handkerchief, however, use a rolled hem. This can be worked by machine and hand, or entirely by machine using a narrow foot hemmer.

Fringing a shawl

Purchase sufficient fringing sold by the metre/yard to go round two sides of a triangle and four sides of a square shawl, allowing extra for turnings and to ease round corners. Pick a colour that complements the shawl background or tones with the painting and ensure that the fringe has a braid edge about 1 cm/½ in wide.

Turn under a narrow hem to the wrong side all round the edges of the shawl and machine stitch. When working corners, trim them off to avoid excessive bulk, then fold one hem over the other when stitching and oversew the edges together by hand, (Fig a).

Tack or pin the braid edge of the fringing in place on the right side of the shawl, either easing the edge in a curve round the corners, or folding one edge under the other to give a mitred effect. Stitch the fringe in place.

Machine rolled hem

This requires a special machine foot and a little practice.

Trim the edges of the shawl or scarf to make sure they are perfectly straight, allowing a 1 cm/½ in hem. Fold under a double hem to the wrong side and work a few machine stitches through the hem. Leave the needle in the fabric and lift the machine foot. Feed the fold of the fabric through the spiral of the hemmer foot, then lower the foot and continue stitching, pulling the fabric taut as you go, (Fig b).

Hand rolled hem

Make sure the edges of the silk are straight, allowing 1 cm/½ in for the finished hem. Work a staystitch by hand, or with small machine stitches, 3 mm/⅛ in from the raw edges all round the scarf or handkerchief. Trim away the fabric to within a few threads of the staystitch, (Fig c).

Turn the full hem allowance to the wrong side and roll the raw edge under so that the line of staystitching just shows. Thread a fine sewing needle with thread of the same colour as the silk and work from right to left along the hem.

Sew along the hem with small, loose blind stitches, (similar to slip stitches), working through the staystitching and the edge of the scarf. Make several stitches and then gently pull up the slack in the thread, causing the edge to roll under, (Fig d). Do not press the edges, which should be left softly rounded to give the hem its characteristic appearance.

Opposite: this striking triangular shawl has a black background and is edged with dramatic black fringing. See overleaf for instructions and chart.

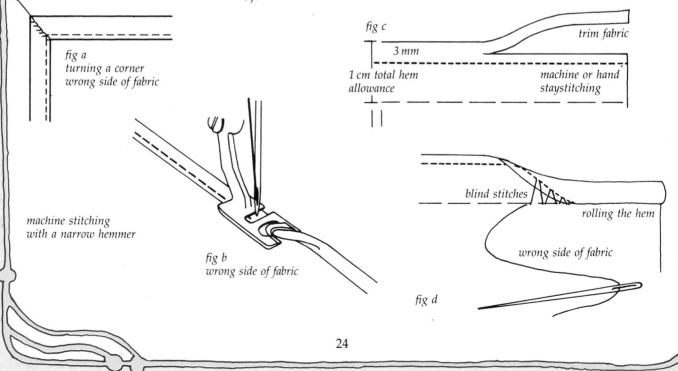

fig a
turning a corner
wrong side of fabric

machine stitching
with a narrow hemmer

fig b
wrong side of fabric

fig c
3 mm
1 cm total hem
allowance
trim fabric
machine or hand
staystitching

blind stitches
rolling the hem
wrong side of fabric

fig d

Black shawl with fringe

This shawl, excluding fringe, measures 120 cm/47¼ in from point to point and 55 cm/21¾ in deep, when completed.

Materials
Fabric: rectangle of silk crêpe 122 cm/48 in wide by 112 cm/44 in long; fringing 150 cm/59 in long.

Paints: black, yellow, lime green, brown and combinations of these colours but not diluted.

Gutta: clear yellow, a little yellow printing ink.

Method examples
Pull the silk rectangle over the frame and draw a triangle using pencil but don't cut out.

Shade the flowers, tree and leaves. Paint the background and cut the silk once the paint is fixed

Machine the hem, sewing on the fringe at the same time along two side edges.

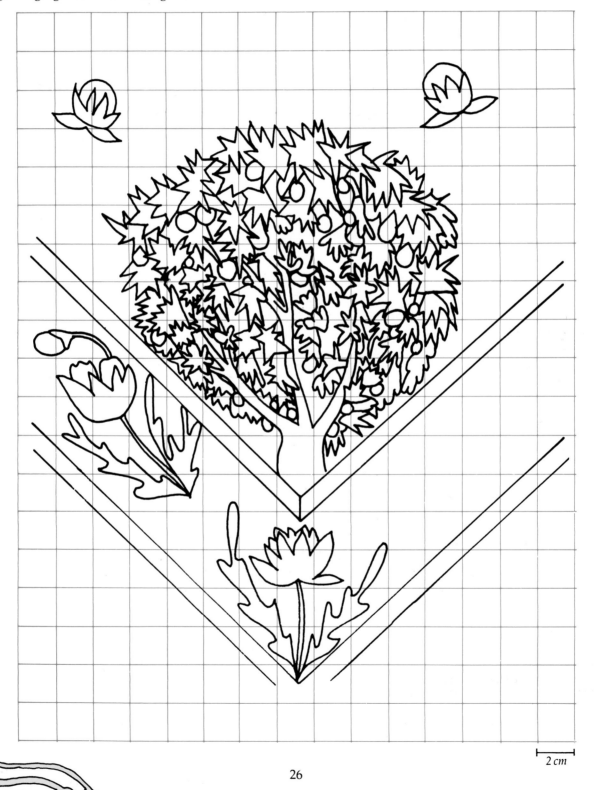

2 cm

Above: *a simple triangular shawl decorated with delicate blossoms and trimmed with silk fringing. The matching skirt can be made from a rectangle of fabric, gathered on to a waistband. See overleaf for instructions and charts.*

White shawl, skirt and top

The shawl, excluding fringe, measures 160 cm/63 in from point to point; the hem of the skirt measures 190 cm/75 in and the length is adjustable; the top can be made to fit any bust size.

Materials

Fabric: silk tussah, rectangle of 92 cm/36 in by 162 cm/64 in for the shawl; width of 192 cm/76 in for skirt, length to suit your height; width of about 104 to 112 cm/41 to 44 in for top; white fringing 250 cm/99 in long.

Paints: rust, cyclamen, crimson, burgundy, violet, yellow, old gold, beige, ochre, brown green, jade, lime green and combinations of these colours as well as diluted versions.

Gutta: colourless, or tinted slightly with yellow.

Method examples

Shawl: draw a triangle within the rectangle using a pencil, but don't cut out. Shade the flowers and leaves well. Cut the silk once it is painted and fixed. Machine the hem, sewing on the fringe at the same time along two side edges.

Skirt: cut the silk to the required size, leaving a length for a waistband. Allowing for the hem, paint the border round the lower edge.

Join centre back seam, make small darts around the top edge to fit waist size and attach the waistband. Handsew lower hem.

Top: cut 2 pieces to fit bust size, allowing for seams. Paint a small motif on the centre front.

Join side seams, hem top and lower edge. Cut and sew on straps to top edge.

chart for skirt

centre of skirt

8 cm

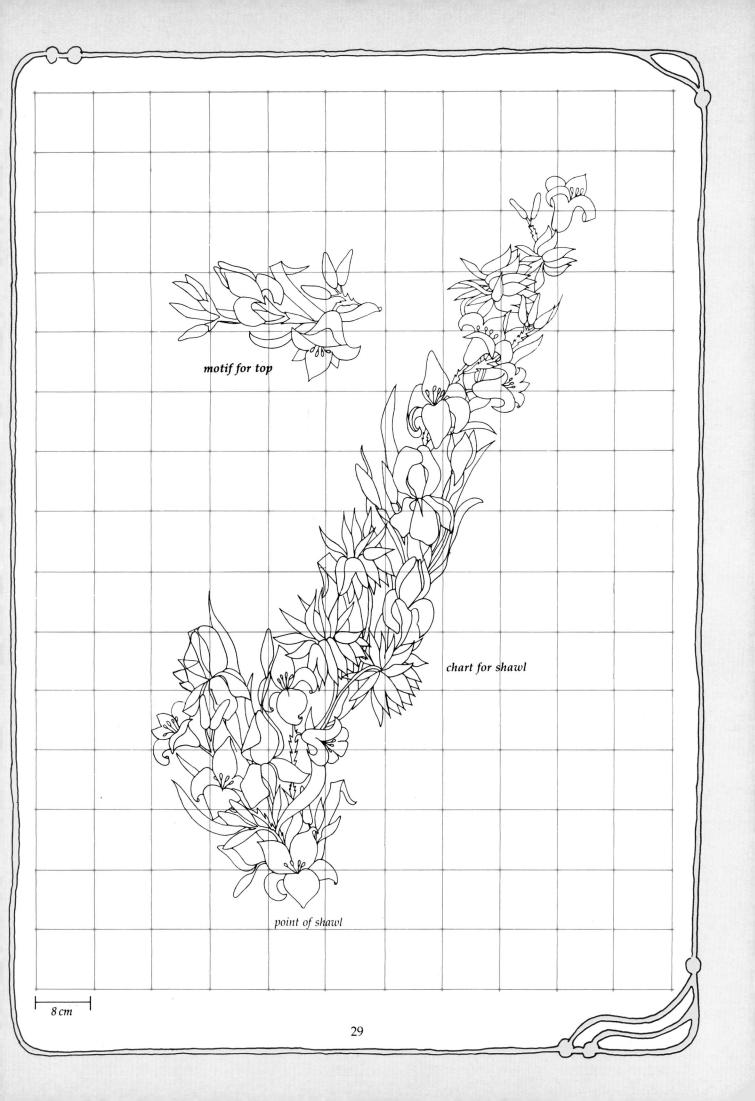

motif for top

chart for shawl

point of shawl

8 cm

Shawl with landscape border

This shawl measures 90 cm/35½ in square. The edges are left unhemmed and slightly frayed but you can finish them by hand, or machine, if preferred.

Materials

Fabric: silk pongé 9, 90 cm/35½ in square.

Paints: cobalt blue, lemon yellow, yellow gold, vermilion red, crimson, burnt sienna, black, rose and combinations of these colours as well as diluted versions.

Gutta: colourless.

Method examples

Paint the border motifs along two edges and the single motif in the remaining corner. Mix the colours well; use darker tones for the shadowed areas and shade well.

For the dappled sky, apply clean alcohol to the white silk background and before it dries, apply a mixture of cobalt blue and alcohol in the shape of clouds, blurring the contours of the alcohol to soften the effect. You must work fast because the alcohol dries very quickly.

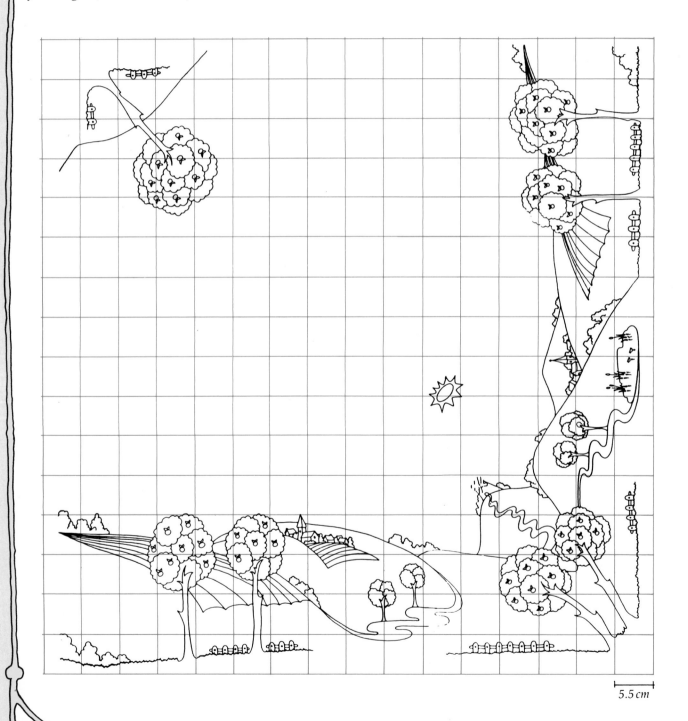

5.5 cm

Sunrise shawl

This shawl measures 90 cm/35½ in square. The edges are left unhemmed and slightly frayed but you can finish them by hand, or machine, if preferred.

Materials
Fabric: silk pongé 9, 90 cm/35½ in square.

Paints: cobalt blue, lemon yellow, yellow gold, vermilion, crimson, burnt sienna, black, rose and combinations of these colours as well as diluted versions.

Gutta: colourless.

Method examples
Apply the gutta and then the paints in very diluted tones for the foreground and in darker tones for the flowers, trees and the details in the foreground.

For the dappled sky, apply clean alcohol to the white silk background and before it dries, apply a mixture of cobalt blue and alcohol in the shape of clouds, blurring the contours of the alcohol to soften the effect. You must work fast because the alcohol dries very quickly.

5 cm

Flower scarf or cushion

This bold flower design can be used for a scarf or a cushion. The finished size of the scarf is 90 cm/35½ in square, and the cushion 46 cm/18 in.

Materials

Fabric: silk crêpe, 91 cm/36 in square for the scarf; silk pongé 5, 48 cm/19 in square for the cushion front.

Opposite: use this motif for an elegant scarf or colourful cushion.

Paints: for the scarf, old gold, rust, ruby red, brown, tobacco brown, jade, duck egg blue, lime green, black, chrome yellow and combinations of these colours.

For the cushion, old gold, yellow gold, chrome yellow, rust, brown, tobacco brown, black as well as diluted versions.

Gutta: black.

Method examples

For the scarf or cushion, apply the gutta with a paintbrush for thick, modulated brushstrokes. You will have to dilute the gutta a little more than usual. Test first on a piece of silk.

For the wide border of the scarf use tobacco brown plus a dot each of ruby red and chrome yellow to make ochre. To make a darker ochre, use the same colours plus a little black and lime green. For orange-gold, mix ruby red and old gold and for green, duck egg blue, jade and a little black.

For the cushion, use the colours pure or diluted but not mixed. Omit the border. See page 38 for making up details.

├─┤ 3 cm
size for the cushion

├────┤ 6 cm
size for the scarf

Long scarf in geometric design

This scarf measures 42 cm/16½ in wide and 140 cm/55¼ in long when finished.

Materials

Fabric: silk crêpe, 142 cm/56 in long by 45 cm/17¾ in wide.

Paints: poppy red, tangerine, old gold, chrome yellow, azure blue, duck egg blue, black, tobacco brown and combinations of these colours as well as diluted versions.

Gutta: pale yellow.

Method examples

Prepare several pots of pure colours, also mix some together and dilute others to give as wide a range of shades as possible.

the chart shows half of the design

8 cm

36

Leopard print scarf

This scarf measures 42 cm/16½ in wide and 140 cm/55¼ in long when finished. No gutta is needed as the colours run into each other.

Materials

Fabric: silk pongé 9, 142 cm/56 in long by 45 cm/17¾ in wide.

Paints: yellow gold, old gold, shell, caramel, and combinations of these colours as well as diluted versions.

Method examples

Stretch the silk and apply a very pale caramel background colour. Leave to dry.

Paint large rings in a darker colour and fill in with a deep caramel brown. Work over the entire area again with a different colour and a mixture of water and alcohol, half-and-half. Leave to dry thoroughly.

Lavender bags and cushions

Luxurious cushions are practical yet ornamental furnishings and need not be expensive. Hand-painted cushions will add the finishing touch to any room and highlight a colour scheme. Even if you are not an experienced needlewoman, making a cushion presents few problems but if you are reluctant to tackle one as your first experiment, try one of the delightful lavender bags given in this section.

First determine the size of the cushion you wish to make; 46 cm/18 in square is a popular size. You will need sufficient silk for the painted front of the cushion and a similar amount for the plain back, allowing extra for seaming.

Ready-made pads to fit inside the cushion cover are available in different sizes and shapes from most furnishing departments. For a lavender bag, you will first have to make a lining to the same shape and fill this with dried lavender flowers. Allow the same amount of fine white cotton, or muslin, as for the silk.

Making a cushion cover
Place the completed silk painting and the remaining piece of silk together, with the right sides facing each other. Tack along three

of the sides of a square, or three-quarters of the way round any other shape, about 1 cm/½ in from the edge. Insert the cushion pad very gently and check that it will fit snugly – if not, retack the seams.

Seam the edges by machine, or by hand using small, neat backstitches. Unpick the tacking stitches. Turn the cover right side out and insert the cushion pad. To close the remaining opening, turn 1 cm/½ in along both edges to the wrong side and either insert a fine zip fastener, or slip stitch the edges together.

To give a perfect fit at the corners of a square cushion cover, the seams should be trimmed off. This will ensure that there are no unsightly lumps of fabric. Before closing the last seam, trim each corner diagonally across, (Fig a). Take care not to cut too close to the stitches.

Adding a frill
You will need sufficient background fabric to give a depth of 10 cm/4 in, making a double frill 5 cm/2 in deep. To gather up the material allow a length which will go round all the outer edges, plus half of this amount again.

Join the fabric in strips to give

the correct length, then join the last two edges together. Fold in half and use small running stitches through both the raw edges to gather up the frill. Have the right side of the cushion back and the raw edges of the frill facing you, and tack the frill in place round all the edges of the cushion as you go, making sure the frill is evenly spaced and easing it in place round corners, (Fig b).

Place the right side of the front of the cushion face down on top of the frill and backing and complete as given for making a cushion.

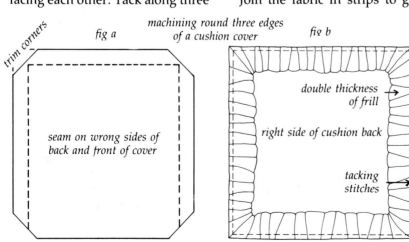

trim corners

fig a

machining round three edges of a cushion cover

fig b

seam on wrong sides of back and front of cover

double thickness of frill

right side of cushion back

tacking stitches

Opposite: *the four seasons. A motif depicting Spring decorates this card-backed and braid-edged wall hanging; seen here with a cushion which features the same motif. See following pages for instructions and charts*

Four seasons pictures

Each picture measures 33 cm/13 in wide and 27 cm/10¾ in deep when finished.

Materials

Fabric: silk pongé 9, 35 cm/13¾ in wide by 30 cm/11¾ in deep for each picture; 125 cm/49¼ in of narrow braid in either moss green, beige, old rose or grey; piece of clear plastic and firm cardboard 33 cm/13 in wide by 27 cm/10¾ in deep.

Method examples

For each picture, place the silk on the frame. Roll some cottonwool round a stick or around the end of a paintbrush, so you don't damage the brush, and dip in anti-fusant already prepared, or a mixture of 20% gutta and 80% spirit. Dampen the silk all over.

When completely dry, trace the drawing on to the silk with Indian ink using a tubular nib, then paint as if on drawing paper, using a very fine paintbrush.

Once the silk has been steamed to fix it, paint a frame to enclose the motif with gold fabric paint, as shown, and fix with an iron.

Four seasons cushions

Each cushion measures 41 cm/16¼ in square when finished.

Materials

Fabric: silk crêpe de chine, 45 cm/17¾ in square for the front of each cushion. Allow same amount of silk or sateen for each back.

Method examples

To match the cushions to the pictures, enlarge the respective design. For the squirrel and grapes design, shown on page 43, replace the squirrel motif with a leaf.

Swallows and magnolias

This design represents 'Spring', see page 39 for illustration.

Materials

Paints: black, dark blue, burgundy, jade, yellow gold, chestnut brown, bright red and combinations of these colours as well as diluted versions, also gold fabric paint.

Gutta: light brown and black.

Method examples

Once you have steamed the painted silk to fix the paints, add the frame using gold fabric paint and fix by ironing.

Stick the silk to the plastic, and stiffen by sticking cardboard on the back for the picture. Add the border of grey braid.

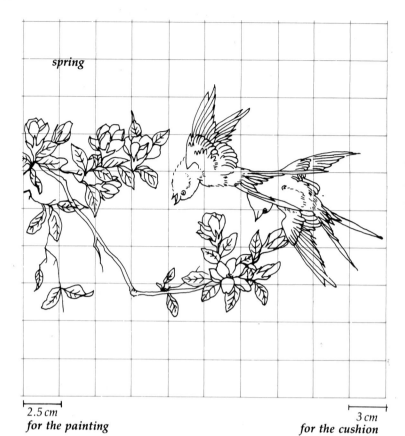

spring

2.5 cm
for the painting

3 cm
for the cushion

Bird and rose

This design represents 'Summer' see page 42 for illustration.

Materials

Paints: ruby red, black, lime green, yellow gold, chestnut brown and combinations of these colours as well as diluted versions, also gold fabric paint.

Gutta: pink, green and brown.

Method examples

Paint the leaves in a range of greens, mixing them with yellow. Use mixtures of chestnut brown and black for the bird, and ruby red and yellow gold tones for the flowers.

Complete the picture as for 'Spring', adding old rose braid.

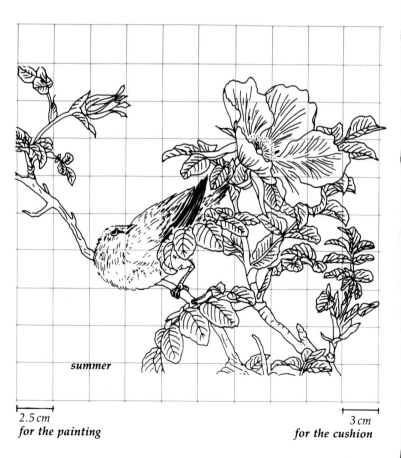

summer

2.5 cm
for the painting

3 cm
for the cushion

Squirrel with grapes

This design represents 'Autumn', see page 43 for illustration.

Materials

Paints: burgundy, tobacco brown, yellow gold, lime green, dark blue, moss green and combinations of these colours as well as diluted versions, also gold fabric paint.

Gutta: brown and green.

Method examples

Darken the leaves and grapes, using the corresponding colour pure. Leave one side of the grapes lighter, to give the impression of a sphere.

Complete the picture as for 'Spring', adding moss green or brown braid.

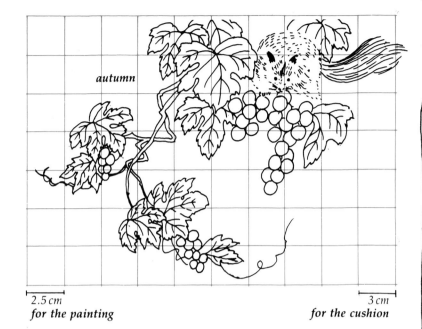

autumn

2.5 cm
for the painting

3 cm
for the cushion

Sparrow and narcissi

This design represents 'Winter', see page 7 for illustration.

Materials

Paints: jade, black, orange, lime green, chestnut brown and combinations of these colours as well as diluted versions, also gold fabric paint.

Gutta: pale green and brown.

Method examples

Paint the background in pale grey-green, mixing jade and very diluted black, leaving some white areas for the snow. Also leave the veins of the leaves and flower petals white.

Complete the picture as for 'Spring', adding beige braid.

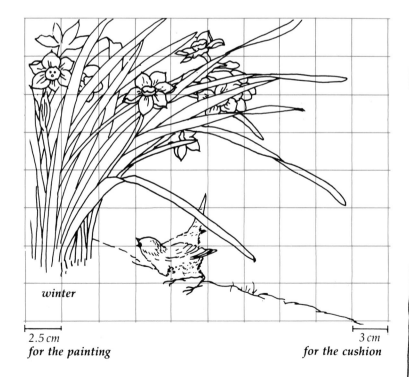

winter

2.5 cm
for the painting

3 cm
for the cushion

Flower cushion

This cushion measures 45 cm/17¾ in square when completed.

Materials

Fabric: silk pongé 5, 47 cm/18½ in square for the cushion front.

Paints: bright pink, ruby red, burgundy, chrome yellow, yellow gold, jade, lime green, cornflower blue, amethyst, brown and combinations of these colours as well as diluted versions.

Gutta: pale green, black and yellow.

Method examples

This design is quite fine and intricate, so keep the gutta lines thin and precise.

Leave the daisies white, just barely tinted with yellow green and shade all the flowers and leaves well.

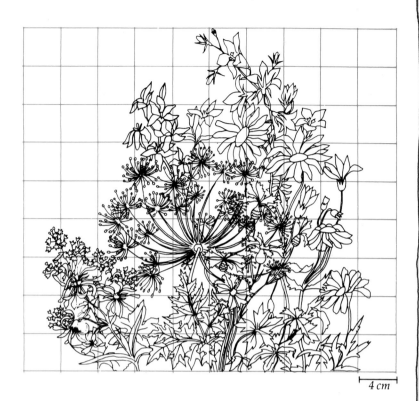

4 cm

46

Fruit and flower cushion

This cushion measures 45 cm/17¾ in square when completed.

Materials

Fabric: silk pongé 5, 47 cm/18½ in square, for the cushion front.

Paints: bright pink, burgundy, ruby red, brown, amethyst, azure blue, navy blue, black, turquoise, tangerine, yellow gold, chrome yellow, old gold, duck egg blue and combinations of these colours as well as diluted versions.

Gutta: colourless, light orange, grey-blue.

Method examples

For the fruit, lighten some of the grapes with a comma-shaped dot of colourless gutta. Shade the other fruits, leaving the colour lighter on the right-hand side.

For the flowers, shade well and paint the veins on the tulip, when

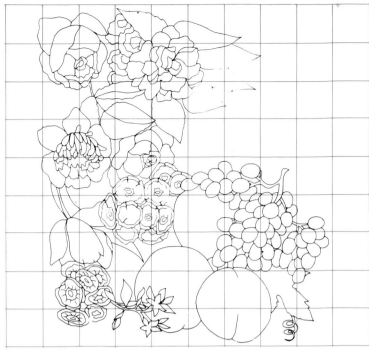

4.5 cm

dry, with a brush dipped in alcohol.

For the background, use the same colours as for the fruit and flowers. Apply the paint in diffe-

rent sized patches and scatter on some coarse salt. When the surface is thoroughly dry, draw in the leaves with a paintbrush dipped in alcohol.

Cyclamen cushion

This cushion measures 42 cm/ 16½ in square when completed.

Materials

Fabric: crêpe de chine, 44 cm/ 17¼ in square, for cushion front.

Paints: black, ruby red, lime green, moss green, chestnut brown and combinations of these colours as well as diluted versions.

Gutta: black, pale grey.

Method examples

Only use the black gutta for the frame around the design.

Paint the flowers in ruby red mixed with a little lime green and shade well.

For the leaves, dampen the areas that remain very pale with pure water first, then paint over the top.

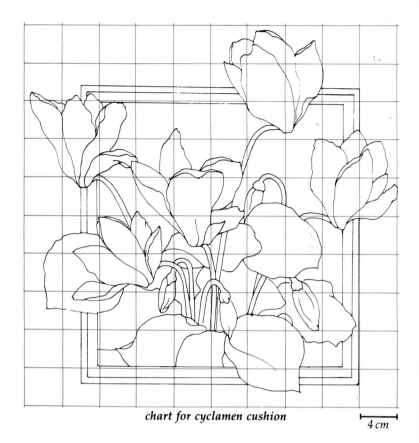

chart for cyclamen cushion　　　⊢——⊣ 4 cm

Tulips and irises cushion

This cushion measures 42 cm/ 16½ in square when completed.

Materials

Fabric: crêpe de chine, 44 cm/ 17¼ in square, for cushion front.

Paints: black, ruby red, chrome yellow, jade, lime green, tobacco brown and combinations of these colours as well as diluted versions.

Gutta: black, pale grey.

Method examples

Only use the black gutta for the frame around the design.

Leave the irises white, shaded with some very diluted lime green and shade all the flowers and leaves well.

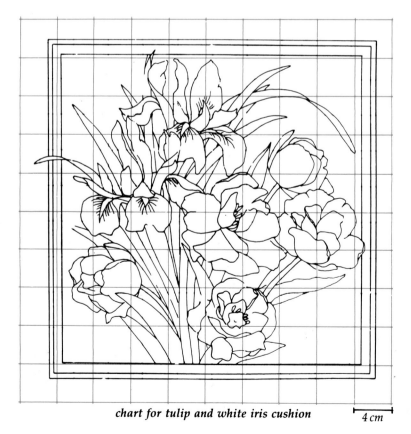

chart for tulip and white iris cushion　　　⊢——⊣ 4 cm

Grey lavender bag

This lavender bag measures 20 cm/7¾ in square, excluding frill, when completed.

Materials

Fabric: silk pongé 5, 21 cm/8¼ in square for bag; 120 cm/47¼ in long by 5 cm/2 in wide for frill; dried lavender.

Paints: black, navy blue, crimson, burgundy, cyclamen, ochre, rust, yellow, lime green, green, jade and combinations of these colours as well diluted versions.

Gutta: light yellow and a little pale yellow printing ink.

Method examples

For the background and frill use a little black and navy blue plus water and alcohol.

Use mixtures of all the other colours for the flowers, lightening them with water and alcohol.

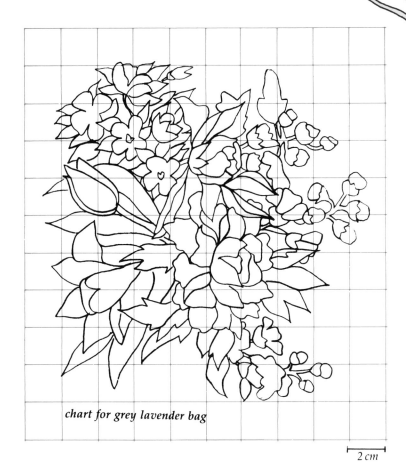

chart for grey lavender bag

2 cm

Pink lavender bag

This lavender bag measures 20 cm/7¾ in square, excluding frill, when completed.

Materials

Fabric: silk pongé 5, 21 cm/8¼ in square for bag; 120 cm/47¼ in long by 5 cm/2 in for frill; dried lavender.

Paints: cyclamen, crimson, violet, ochre, yellow, old gold, brown, lime green, jade, green and combinations of these colours as well as diluted versions.

Gutta: light grey and a little black printing ink.

Method examples

For the background and frill use cyclamen plus water and alcohol.

Use mixtures of all the colours for the flowers, lightening them with water and alcohol.

chart for pink lavender bag

2cm

Lavender bags

The boy measures 19 cm/7¼ in high by 11 cm/4¼ in wide when completed; the girl 23 cm/9 in high by 14 cm/5½ in wide and the square bag 20 cm/7¾ in square.

Materials

Fabric: silk pongé 5; for the boy 21 cm/8¼ in by 13 cm/5 in; for the girl 25 cm/9¾ in by 16 cm/6¼ in; for the square 22 cm/8¾ in square; dried lavender.

Paints: for the boy vermilion, yellow, turquoise; for the girl yellow, old gold, vermilion, azure blue; for the square azure blue, turquoise, jade, vermilion, green, ochre, old gold, yellow.

For all models, combinations of the colours as well as diluted versions.

Gutta: for the boy, black, blue-grey, blue, black printing ink; for the girl black, light yellow; for the square grey, black printing ink.

Method examples

The boy's eyes and hair are painted with printing ink, also the hair on the square bag.

Paint the girl's features when the background is wet, also boy's.

2 cm

Accessories and neckties

Hand-painted pure silk handkerchiefs and accessories, such as belts, bags or small cases, form most attractive gifts and are simple and inexpensive to make. For the man in your life, or as a colourful addition to your own wardrobe, a luxurious silk necktie would be an accessory to treasure!

Guidelines for assembling the accessories shown on pages 57 and 59 are given in this section, and details of how to hem a handkerchief can be found on page 24. Helpful hints on how to make a necktie are also given here, but if you are not an experienced dressmaker it would be wise to buy a suitable paper pattern.

Making a necktie
The sections of painted silk and interlining must be cut on the cross from single pieces of fabric. Allow sufficient material to enable the pieces to be cut on the bias at an angle of 45°. Because of the length of the sections, you will need at least 1 m/1 yd of 91 cm/36 in wide fabric.

Allow extra silk to match patterned or striped fabrics and note that diagonal patterns are unsuitable, as when the fabric is cut on the cross they will become vertical, or horizontal, depending on the direction of the pattern.

On the diagrams shown here, a seam allowance of 10 mm/⅜ in has already been added to all pieces.

Cutting the pattern
Cut paper patterns to the measurements shown on the diagram, (Fig a), for each section of silk and interlining. Clearly mark each piece with all the marks and relevant cutting information.

Cut out each piece of fabric and leave it pinned to its own section of the paper pattern.

Assembling the pieces
1) Stitch the wide end of the silk to the neck section, points B to B. Join the narrow end of the silk to the neck section, points A to A. Press seams. (Fig b).

fig b joining the three sections of silk

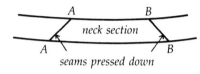

2) Fold corners to right side of fabric and seam the shaped ends of the silk, turning under a 10 mm/⅜ in hem. Press. (Fig c).

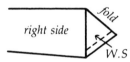

fig c seaming shaped ends of silk

3) Join the 2 sections of interlining C to C. Fold in half lengthways and press. Fold the silk in half lengthways, right sides together, and tack raw edges together.
4) Place the foldline of the interlining over the silk, with the crease over the tacking stitches. Tack these 3 layers together, then seam. Remove tacking stitches. Press open. (Fig d).

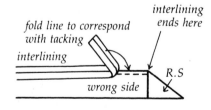

fig d attaching interlining to silk

5) Turn tie right side out and press.

Assembling belts and bags
In addition to the completed silk you will require sufficient polyester padding about 6 mm/¼ in thick, lining fabric, stiff backing material such as fine buckram, thin or thick braid cord and a small amount of glue.

Belts
Cut a paper pattern from the diagrams shown on the relevant pages to the required depth and length to fit your waist size. Using the pattern, cut one piece each of silk, lining, padding and a piece of backing material slightly smaller than the pattern.
1) Glue the padding on to the backing material and leave until completely dry.
2) With right sides together, stitch the silk and lining together, leaving a short section open to allow fabric to be turned inside out. Turn to right side and press lightly.
3) Insert padding and backing between silk and lining and slip stitch opening together.
4) Sew a length of thick cord to each end of the belt to tie at back. Either knot ends or complete with metal tips, available from most craft shops.

Bags and small cases
Cut a paper pattern from the diagrams shown on the relevant page to size and shape required. Using the pattern, cut one piece of silk, three pieces of lining, two pieces of padding and a piece of backing material slightly smaller than the pattern.
1) Glue one piece of padding to the backing material and leave until completely dry.

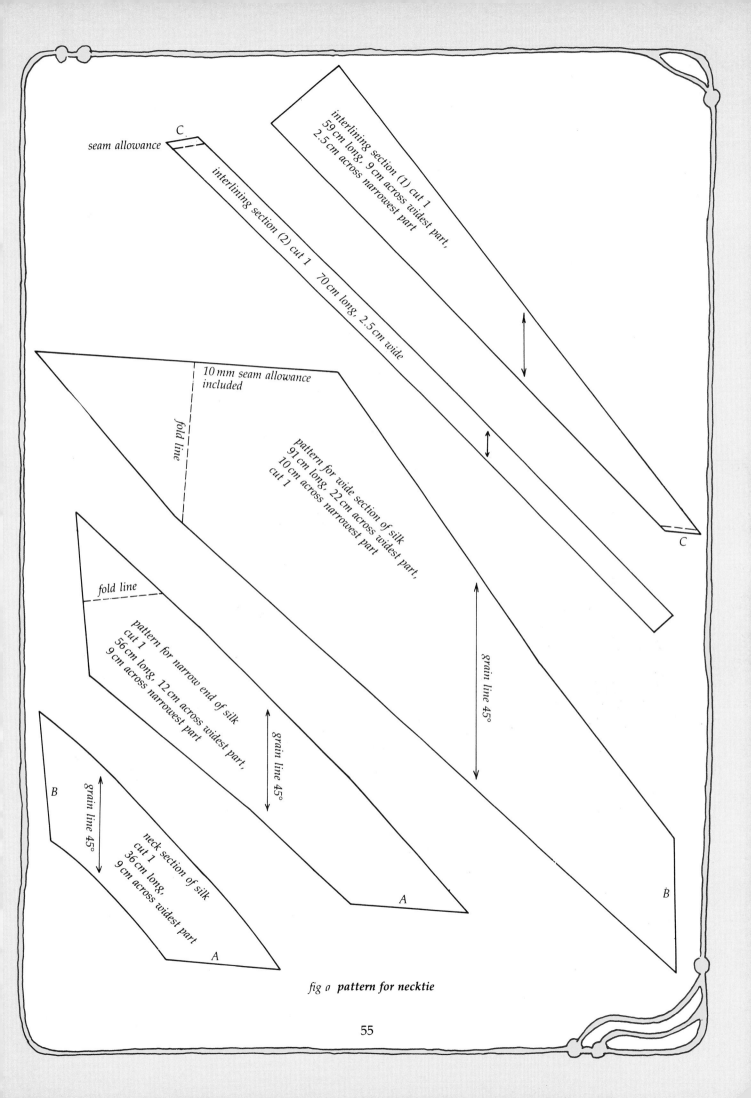

interlining section (1) cut 1
59 cm long, 9 cm across widest part,
2.5 cm across narrowest part

seam allowance

C

interlining section (2) cut 1 70 cm long, 2.5 cm wide

C

10 mm seam allowance
included

fold line

pattern for wide section of silk
91 cm long, 22 cm across widest part,
10 cm across narrowest part
cut 1

grain line 45°

fold line

pattern for narrow end of silk
cut 1
56 cm long, 12 cm across widest part,
9 cm across narrowest part

grain line 45°

A

B

B

grain line 45°

neck section of silk
cut 1
36 cm long,
9 cm across widest part

A

fig a **pattern for necktie**

55

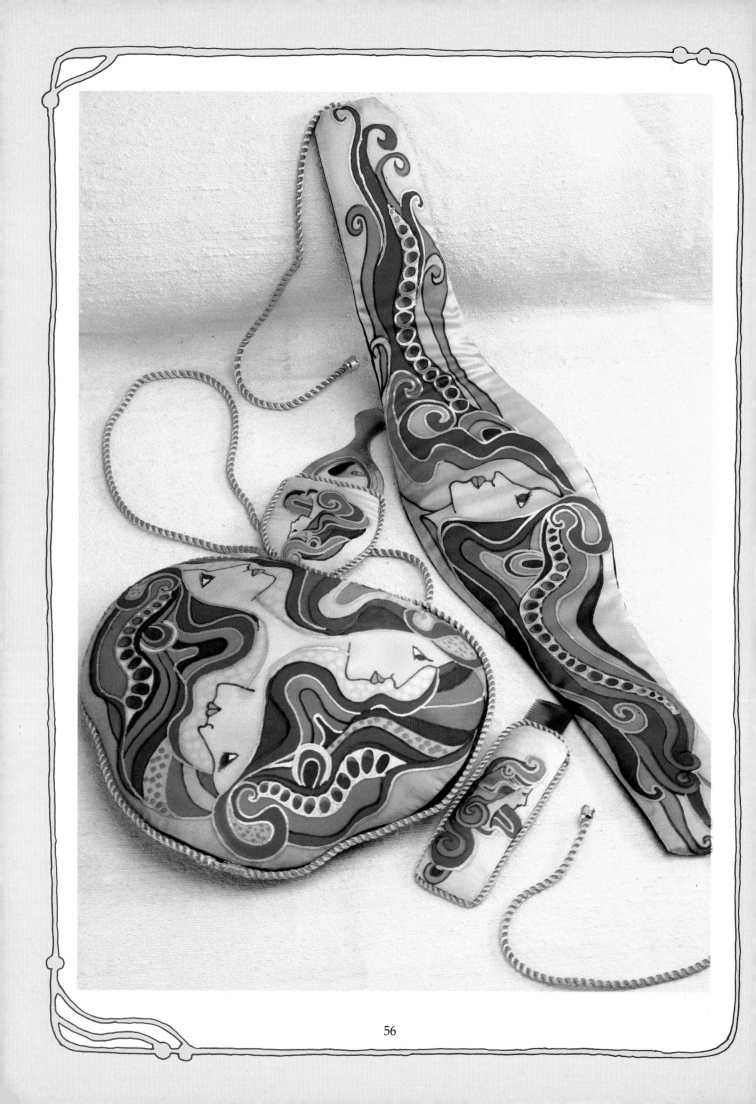

2) With right sides together, stitch the silk and one piece of lining together, leaving top edge open. Repeat with remaining two pieces of lining. Turn each section to right side and press lightly.

3) Slip the padding and backing material into the silk and lining section. Adjust to fit and join open edge with blind stitch.

4) Slip remaining piece of padding into the lining section. Adjust to fit and join open edge with blind stitch.

5) Stitch both sections together by hand, using small, neat oversewing stitches and leave an opening at the top edge.

6) To complete a bag, place the ends of a length of cord sufficient to go over the shoulder between the top edges and stitch firmly.

For small comb or mirror cases, blind stitch thin cord around all edges.

Accessories with face motifs

These accessories can be adjusted to suit your own measurements.

Materials

Fabric: silk twill, 50 cm/19¾ in wide by 70 cm/27½ in long for the set.

Paints: azure blue, cornflower blue, navy blue, duck egg blue, black, pink, yellow gold, tobacco brown and combinations of these colours as well as diluted versions.

Gutta: black and gold.

Method examples

To colour the faces, use very diluted tobacco brown mixed with yellow gold. Put a spot of pale pink on the cheeks while still wet.

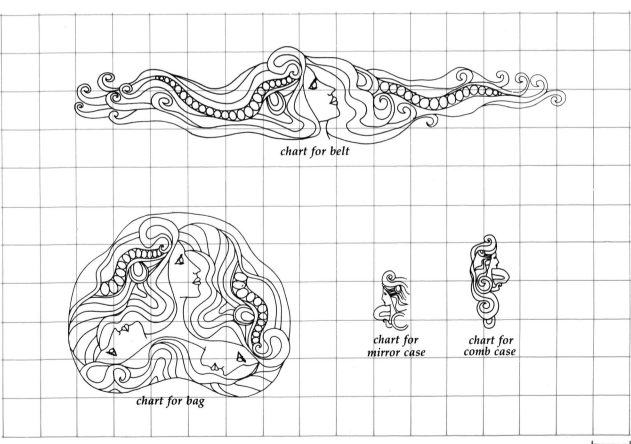

chart for belt

chart for bag

chart for mirror case

chart for comb case

5 cm

Opposite: a selection of useful accessories, comprising a belt, and bag, comb and mirror cases.

Accessories with birds motifs

These accessories can be adjusted to suit your own measurements.

Materials

Fabric: silk pongé 9, 50 cm/19¾ in wide by 70 cm/27½ in long for the set.

Paints: burgundy, tangerine, yellow gold, old gold, lime green, jade, black, azure blue, duck egg blue, cornflower blue, navy blue, tobacco brown and combinations of these colours as well as diluted versions.

Gutta: blue.

Method examples

Shade the feathers well. Leave a little white near the head. While still damp, spot the surface of the neck with grey and duck egg blue.

chart for bag

chart for comb case

chart for glasses case

chart for mirror case

chart for belt

5 cm

Opposite: *these accessories feature a colourful bird motif. They include a belt, bag, comb and mirror cases and also a spectacle case.*

Blue striped and mottled ties

Each tie measures 140 cm/55 in long when completed.

Materials

Fabric: for each tie, wild silk or crêpe, 80 cm/31½ in long by 56 cm/22 in wide; interlining 71 cm/28 in long by 25 cm/9¾ in wide.

Paints: blue striped tie burgundy, navy blue, azure blue; mottled tie azure blue, grey, burgundy and combinations of these colours as well as diluted versions.

Gutta: striped tie, dark grey.

Method examples

For the striped tie, draw stripes of unequal width with gutta across the grain of the fabric. Spot some of the stripes with coarse salt and others with alcohol.

No gutta is needed for mottled tie. Wet the silk well and apply the colours well diluted. Sprinkle with a little coarse salt.

Tie and handkerchief sets

Each tie measures 140 cm/55 in long and each handkerchief 23 cm/9 in square, or size required, when completed.

Materials

Fabric: for each set, wild silk or crêpe, 80 cm/31½ in long by 56 cm/22 in wide for the tie and 26 cm/10¼ in square for the handkerchief; interlining for each tie 71 cm/28 in long by 25 cm/9¾ in wide.

Paints: for the set with centre motifs, tobacco brown for the background, orange, old gold, brown, yellow gold; for the patterned set, lime green, old gold, brown, rust, tobacco brown and combinations of these colours as well as diluted versions.

Gutta: for the set with centre motifs, black; for the patterned set, orange.

Method examples

The set with centre motifs is very simple. Apply the background with a soft brush.

Apply the outlines of the design for the patterned set as you wish,

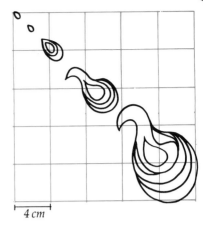

4 cm

making freehand circular shapes. Paint inside the areas created, leaving some white.

61

Geometric tie and handkerchief

The tie measures 140 cm/55 in long and the handkerchief 23 cm/9 in square, or size required, when completed.

Materials
Fabric: silk satin, 80 cm/31½ in long by 56 cm/22 in wide for the tie and 26 cm/10¼ in square for the handkerchief; interlining for the tie 71 cm/28 in long by 25 cm/9¾ in wide.

Paints: burgundy, duck egg blue, lime green, black and combinations of these colours as well as diluted versions.

Gutta: grey-green, black, silver.

Method examples
Only part of the chart is shown as it is better to execute the design freehand. The geometric shapes are very simple.

The pink, green and duck egg blue area should be lightly softened with grey.

Two ties

Each tie measures 140 cm/55 in long when completed.

Materials

Fabric: silk pongé 10 for each tie, 80 cm/31½ in long by 56 cm/22 in wide; interlining 71 cm/28 in long by 25 cm/9¾ in wide.

Paints: for both ties, burgundy, black, petrol blue, old gold, tobacco brown, brown, tangerine and combinations of these colours as well as diluted versions.

Gutta: grey.

Method examples

For the tie with the central motif, use burgundy with a little black, well diluted with water and alcohol for the background. Shade the design from pale blue to light blue-grey, then to dark grey.

For the patterned tie, use all the colours diluted, keeping the diagonal stripes darker. Use old gold diluted with water and alcohol for the background.

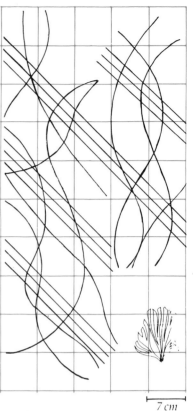

7 cm

3 cm

Handkerchief with festoon border

This handkerchief measures 28 cm/11 in square when completed.

Materials

Fabric: silk pongé 9, 30 cm/11¾ in square.

Paints: fuchsia, ruby red, lime green, moss green, duck egg blue, royal blue and combinations of these colours as well as diluted versions.

Gutta: colourless.

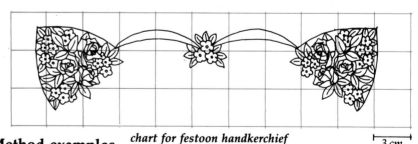

chart for festoon handkerchief

⊢——⊣ 3 cm

Method examples

Paint the border and roses in a mixture of fuchsia and ruby red and the small flowers in duck egg and royal blue monochrome. For the scallops, use a mixture of duck egg and royal blue.

Hand, or machine-roll the hem, see page 24.

Handkerchief with roses motif

This handkerchief measures 30 cm/11¾ in square when completed.

Materials

Fabric: silk pongé 9, 32 cm/12½ in square.

Paints: black, ruby red, fuchsia, moss green, duck egg blue and combinations of these colours as well as diluted versions.

Gutta: pale grey.

Method examples

Paint the background in well-diluted black, to give pale grey.

Shade the roses well, using the two colours on the border.

Hand, or machine-roll the hem, see page 24.

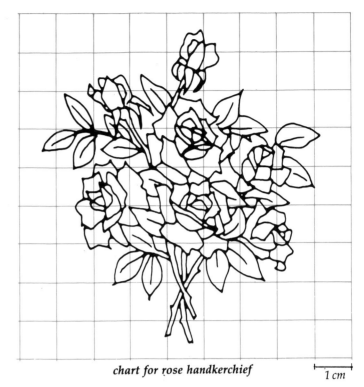

chart for rose handkerchief

⊢——⊣
1 cm

Lily of the valley handkerchief

This handkerchief measures 28 cm/11 in square when completed.

Materials

Fabric: silk pongé 9, 30 cm/11¾ in square.

Paints: orange, lime green, moss green and combinations of these colours as well as diluted versions.

Gutta: pale grey, green.

Method examples

Leave the lace border, ribbon and flowers white. Use slightly lightened orange for the background. The leaves are painted in a mixture of lime and moss green.

Hand, or machine-roll the hem, see page 24.

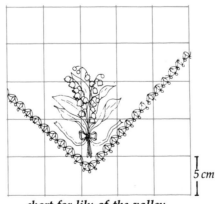

5 cm

chart for lily-of-the-valley handkerchief

Framed paintings

Painting on silk is the ideal way of creating your own original masterpiece, combining unique shapes and blends of colours. It is true to say that no two silk paintings can ever be quite alike and even if you used exactly the same design and colours, you would never be able to repeat the original painting. Silk treated with a film of anti-fusant, see page 87, is the ideal material for a painting.

When you have completed a painting that you intend to display, it will need to be mounted and framed. Most art shops will undertake this process for you but if you prefer to complete the whole project yourself, you can obtain the necessary materials and equipment from the same source.

Before beginning to paint, there are one or two points to consider. Such a painting will obviously have pride of place in your home, so choose a subject in keeping with the ambiance of the room in which the picture will be displayed. A delicate subject in soft colours, for example, would not be out of place in a very feminine bedroom but would be lost in a room with a more masculine emphasis. Use colours which will complement the decor of the room. When the picture is framed under glass, any reflected light may distort the colours slightly. Although it may be a little more expensive, it is best to use a non-reflective glass.

Picture frames

The diagram, (Fig a), shows the components that go to make up the mount, backing and frame. Either purchase a frame which includes all these parts, or assemble them separately. Old frames are very attractive and can sometimes be picked up very cheaply at jumble sales but the backing and mounting materials will probably need replacing.

Backing board

Glazed frames require a firm backing to hold the painting rigid and to keep out dust. The most suitable material is hardboard but the mouldings on some frames are rather shallow and will not take the thickness of the hardboard. A thin, strong cardboard makes an effective alternative.

Decorative front mount

The painting will not extend to the full area of the material because the silk had to be pinned out on a frame. The unpainted edges will therefore need to be concealed by a cardboard surround. White and coloured mounting boards are available at most art shops. Select a colour which will enhance the painting, without clashing with the decor of the room.

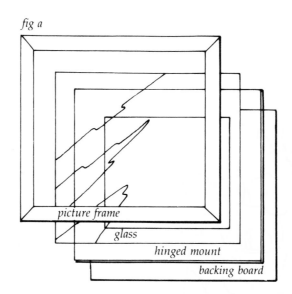

fig a

picture frame

glass

hinged mount

backing board

Opposite: the perfect painting of a rose, elegantly mounted and framed. See overleaf for instructions and chart.

Mounting and framing a painting

Cut a piece of decorative mounting card to the inner measurements of the picture frame and allow an extra 6 mm/¼ in all round to fit into the frame rebate. Cut a backing board to exactly the same size.

Check the area of the painting that needs to be concealed by the decorative mount and pencil in a 'window'. Ensure that this gives a well-balanced sight area of the picture. Use a steel rule and a sharp craft knife to cut out the window. (Fig b)

To complete the mount, join the top edge of the decorative front and the backing together with strong sticky tape. Position the painting on the backing so that the desired area is seen through the window on the front. Use four strips of double-sided sticky tape to attach the picture to the backing at each corner. (Fig c).

Place the mounted painting in the frame face downwards. Pin the hardboard back in place with panel pins, lightly tapped into the inner edges of the frame. Attach picture hooks and cord, or picture wire if the frame is heavy.

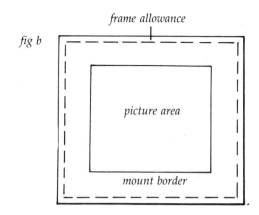

fig b

frame allowance

picture area

mount border

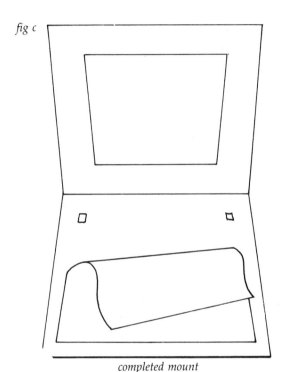

fig c

completed mount

'Roses'

This painting measures 28.5 cm/11¼ in wide by 36.5 cm/14½ in deep when completed.

Materials

Fabric: silk pongé 7, 30 cm/11¾ in wide by 38 cm/15 in deep; 105 cm/41½ in gold braid.

Paints: black, bright red, chrome yellow, lime green, moss green and combinations of these colours as well as diluted versions.

Gutta: colourless.

Method examples

Shade the flowers and leaves well. Use a mixture of all the colours to paint the background.

Edge with gold braid before mounting.

4 cm

'Chrysanthemums'

This painting measures 59 cm/ 23¼ in wide by 49 cm/19¼ in deep when completed.

Materials

Fabric: silk pongé 7, 62 cm/24½ in wide by 52 cm/20½ in deep.

Paints: black, lime green, moss green, chrome yellow, old gold, bright red, tangerine, ruby red, tobacco brown, royal blue and combinations of these colours as well as diluted versions.

Gutta: colourless.

Method examples

Only paint 5 or 6 petals at a time, using the most diluted colour first. While the surface is still damp, superimpose the stronger colour at the base of the petals.

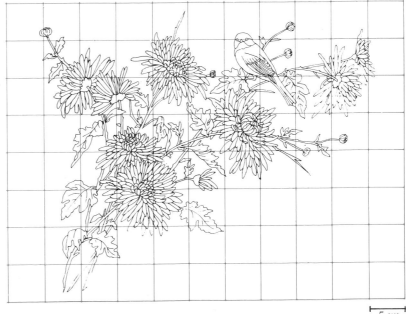

5 cm

'Hibiscus'

This painting measures 40 cm/ 15¾ in wide by 45 cm/17¾ in deep when completed.

Materials

Fabric: silk pongé 7, 43 cm/17 in wide by 48 cm/19 in deep.

Paints: bright red, emerald green, lime green, moss green, cognac, black, tangerine and combinations of these colours as well as diluted versions, also green fabric paint.

Gutta: colourless.

Method examples

Shade the petals well, darkening towards the centre with bright red and black. Using a fine paintbrush, speckle the tip of the stamen with a little printing ink.

Prepare different shades of green from a base of lime green, through emerald and moss green and paint the leaves, darkening some with black and lightening others with emerald.

Paint the bird, outlining the feathers with pure cognac.

Use diluted tangerine for the background. Leave to dry, then draw the grass with fabric paint. Fix this with an iron before fixing the silk.

2 cm

'Peonies'

This painting is after the style of the Japanese painter, Kaiho Yûshô, 1533 to 1615, showing details of a screen painted on paper with gold leaf. It measures 55 cm/21¾ in wide by 75 cm/29½ in deep before framing.

Materials

Fabric: silk pongé 9, 65 cm/25½ in wide by 85 cm/33½ in deep.

Paints: mustard yellow, lime green, navy blue, cobalt blue, caramel, carmine red and combinations of these colours as well as diluted versions.

Gutta: beige and gold.

Method examples

Begin with the background, applying the mustard yellow evenly. Take care not to allow any paint on to the flowers or leaves.

Using a slightly darker tone of mustard, draw regular sized squares on top of the background, with a fine paintbrush dipped in a little paint. Partly shade in the squares to suggest the gold leaf. Accentuate this effect by crayonning in the squares on the left-hand side unevenly with gold gutta and a drawing pen.

For the leaves use a mixture of medium lime green and blue. Shade with caramel. Blend the different tones by alternating with a mixture of water and alcohol to push back the colour and give an impression of depth. Use the same technique for the large stone at the bottom left-hand side of the design, as well as for the red and caramel flowers. Colour only slightly at first, then darken the contours with background paint.

Finish by lightly spraying some blue paint, any colour will do, on to the topmost edge. The idea is to turn the edges of the yellow background green, and so emphasise the centre of the painting.

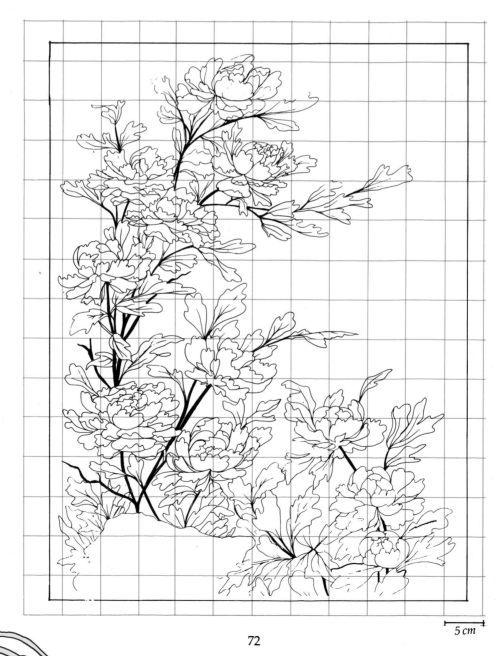

5 cm

Two bird paintings

Each painting measures 44 cm/ 17¼ in wide by 58 cm/22¾ in deep, without the frame.

Materials

Fabric: silk pongé 5, 46 cm/18 in wide by 60 cm/23½ in deep for each painting.

Paints: birds with pink border, pink, ruby red, burgundy, chrome yellow, azure blue, duck egg blue, jade, black, tobacco brown, lime green, tangerine; birds with blue border, pink, chrome yellow, old gold, azure blue, cornflower blue, black, duck egg blue, jade, brown, tobacco brown.

Combinations of these colours as well as diluted versions and anti-fusant for both paintings.

Gutta: beige, yellow, red and green for both paintings.

Method examples

For the birds with the pink border, shade the birds well in green and blue, with a touch of yellow. The crop of the bird at the top is lighter, so before applying the colours, dab a little water on to the crop, then blend the colours on the damp surface. The heads of both birds, and the crop of the lower bird are grey with a few dabs of blue, applied to the surface when still damp.

The foliage is in a range of greens, each leaf lightened with a stroke of yellow. The flowers are shaded in pink, leaving the lighter areas almost white. Add a few strokes of grey and pale yellow.

Paint the rocks in varying shades of grey, coloured with very diluted tangerine, some pink and yellow.

Paint the background in pastel shades, so prepare a variety of very diluted azure blue, pink, tangerine, blue and grey-green. Dampen with water and apply the colours smoothly, letting them blend together. When dry, apply anti-fusant to the entire background. Leave to dry. Paint the border in three shades of burgundy.

For the blue birds, paint the birds in blue monochrome, diluted to varying degrees and using some amounts of grey. Leave some areas white. Add some comma-shaped dots in a brighter colour to the lighter zones to represent the feathers, using the paint sparingly on a dry surface.

Shade the foliage well, painting diagonally from the central veins and varying the colours in bands to represent the ribs. The flowers are pink, shaded with a few drops of yellow.

Paint the background as given for the birds with a pink border. For the border use very diluted azure blue with a little black, and azure blue slightly diluted.

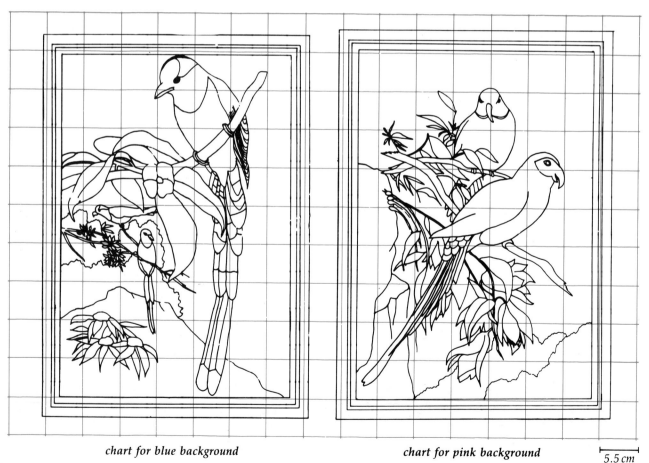

chart for blue background *chart for pink background* 5.5 cm

Autumn landscape

This painting measures 50 cm/19¾ in square, without the frame.

Materials

Fabric: silk pongé 9, 52 cm/20½ in square.

Paints: tangerine, yellow, tobacco brown, sienna, crimson, grey, azure blue, black and combinations of these colours as well as diluted versions, also black Indian ink and anti-fusant.

Method examples

This design does not require any gutta. Draw the main lines on to the silk with a fine pencil, outlining the sky, hills, water and river banks. Paint the background in diluted colours, using orange, yellow and a dot of pink to produce beige for the sky. For the river banks use very diluted beige and orange pastel tones. They will be worked again 'when the anti-fusant has been applied. Don't let the colours merge at the edge of the pond. Use blue-grey tones for the pond and leave some areas almost white.

Apply anti-fusant to the whole surface and when it is dry, work directly with the paints. Begin with the colours for the foliage, hills, river banks and water reflections, using a No 3 paintbrush. Then work on the tree trunks, branches, grasses and the houses with a No 1 paintbrush. Shade the trunks well and finish with a little Indian ink, applied with a fine-nibbed pen to emphasise the relief effect.

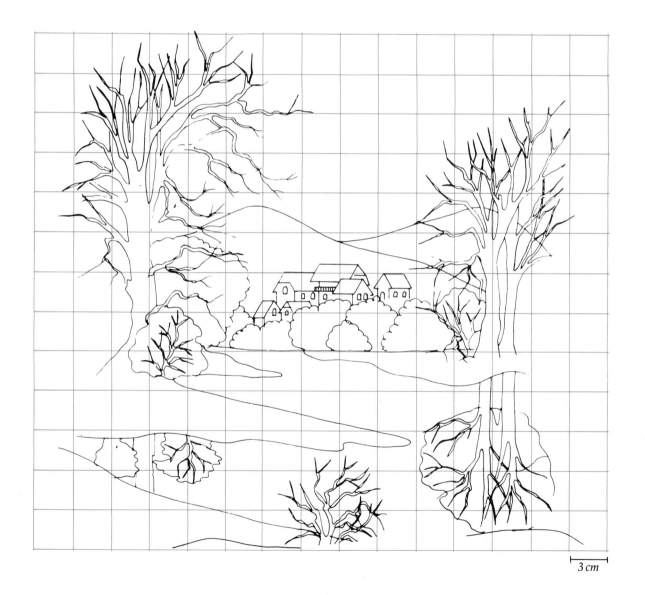

3 cm

76

Painting of a pond

This painting measures 40 cm/ 15¾ in square, without the mount or frame.

Materials

Fabric: silk pongé 5 or 9, 42 cm/ 16½ in square.

Paints: rust, cathedral blue, navy blue, fir green, fern green, turquoise, Parma violet, gold and combinations of these colours as well as diluted versions, also antifusant.

Method examples

Paint the sky and water in very diluted cathedral blue, violet and turquoise. When the paint is dry, trace lines on the water with a fine paintbrush dipped in pure alcohol. Apply an even film of antifusant. Paint the trees using a No 6 stencil brush, dipped in very little paint and apply the colours pure; gold, fir green and rust. Paint the trunks and branches in navy blue -with a No 1 paintbrush.

With a No 2 fan-shaped brush, paint the grass in fir green and rust, then the trees in the distance. Move the paintbrush from bottom to top, dipped in a little pure colour. Add a few houses in rust on the far bank of the pond. Paint the reflections in diluted fern green.

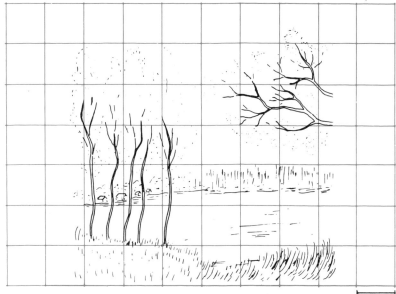

4 cm

Painting of dog roses and bird

This painting measures 49 cm/19¾ in wide by 41 cm/16¼ in deep, without the frame.

Materials

Fabric: wild silk, 51 cm/20 in wide by 43 cm/17 in deep.

Paints: ruby red, burgundy, fuchsia, cornflower blue, chrome yellow, duck egg blue, jade, black, tobacco brown, old gold, lime green and combinations of these colours as well as diluted versions, also white and yellow fabric paint and anti-fusant.

Gutta: green, pink, black.

Method examples

Paint the flowers in tones of diluted ruby red and burgundy, shading well and leaving some white areas on each petal. Paint the leaves in different tones of diluted green, sometimes tinted with a little blue or jade. Add a few spots of pink.

5 cm

For the bird, apply a dot of fuchsia on the head. Keep the chest very pale, slightly coloured with yellow, and the body is bronze with a few dashes of blue. Indicate the wing and tail feathers with cornflower blue.

When the leaves are dry, apply anti-fusant, then paint the veins dark green. When the flowers are dry, paint each petal with a little white fabric paint to make them luminous, and add stamens in yellow fabric paint.

Three sporting paintings

Each painting measures 25 cm/ 9¾ in wide by 21 cm/8¼ in deep, without the frame.

Materials

Fabric: silk pongé 5, 27 cm/10¾ in wide by 23 cm/9 in deep.

Paints: for each painting poppy red, yellow gold, azure blue, cornflower blue, duck egg blue, black, brown, lime green and diluted versions of these colours.

Gutta: colourless.

Method examples

These are easy to paint, as no shading is required. The sky is a mixture of azure blue· and very diluted duck egg blue.

3 cm

How to begin

Once you have mastered the basic technique, this exciting craft can be used to produce luxurious and original designs at relatively low costs.

There are three different methods used in painting on silk; gutta or resist, watercolour, and salt or alcohol techniques. The gutta or resist method can be used on its own to produce very simple, stylised motifs in a single colour. The watercolour method can also be used alone for very muted, abstract designs, where one colour flows into another. Most designs, however, are based on a combination of these first two methods. Salt, or alcohol, is applied to a completed painting to give a stippled effect to certain areas, but these are not used as separate methods. Both agents affect the density of the paint colour; salt will darken it in mottled areas and alcohol lighten it.

Before attempting to paint on silk it is important to appreciate that you will never be able to re-produce an exact replica of any illustrated design. Silk is a natural fibre and, much like wool, varies in quality and texture. For most of the patterns featured in this book we recommend using light weight silks, as these are easier for a beginner to handle and are also less expensive. There is nothing to stop you using a better quality silk, however, but bear in mind that thicker silks demand more care and skill when applying the gutta and paints. Paints may also vary in thickness and colour from one manufacturer to another. Another point to bear in mind is that a design may originally have been drawn free-hand, without any clear lines of reference, so it is a 'one-off', not to be repeated. These factors, however, greatly add to the fascination of this craft, as you will always produce your own unique design.

Make sure you have everything you will require to hand before beginning any project. You will need to work quickly to achieve satisfactory results and if you have to break off in the middle of an operation because you have forgotten to buy a brush fine enough to paint small areas, the whole process could be ruined. You will also need a steady hand and eye, so make sure you are not interrupted once you have commenced a painting!

You need not make any vast initial outlay on tools or materials. Scraps of silk can be found on most remnant counters at prices to suit all purses. Keep to a few basic paint colours for your first project. Don't go to the expense of purchasing a frame for a small item; you may already possess an embroidery frame which would make a suitable alternative. Or, if you can handle a screwdriver, it is a simple matter to make a fixed frame to any size.

Basic equipment

The tools required for painting on silk are easily obtainable from art and craft shops, or by mail order from specialist suppliers. The beginner's kit should contain the following:

A wooden frame, fixed or adjustable

Tracing paper

Silk fabric

Silk paints in two or three colours

Small white mixing cups and container for water

Gutta, or resist agent, or watersolvent resist agent

Paper cones or resist applicators

Gutta or resist colourants, or coloured resist

Thinner and fixing agents, as recommended by the manufacturer of the range of paints being used

Special salt from silk paints suppliers, or fine or coarse cooking salt

Ethyl rubbing alcohol

Two or three soft watercolour-type brushes

Pencil and white eraser fluid

Push pins or three-pointed thumbtacks

Ruler

Adhesive tape

Cotton wool or cotton buds

Scissors

Opposite: some of the basic equipment used in painting on silk.

Tools, materials and basic techniques

This chapter gives details of the items and basic resist and watercolour techniques needed to begin your first venture into silk painting. Any additional material, or special methods needed to complete individual projects featured in this book, will be given in the instructions for the design.

Silk fabrics

Silk is obtained from the cocoon of the wild or cultivated silkworm and, when these are dried, 31 g/ 1 oz will provide sufficient thread for 7 metres/yards of a lightweight fabric 91 cm/36 in wide.

The Chinese have a system of weight gauge for silk, referred to as a 'mommie', and this term is used universally in the wholesale silk trade to indicate the weight of a fabric. One mommie equals 4.3056 gm/⁵⁄₃₂ oz in weight to one square metre/yard of fabric; 6 mommie is considered a lightweight quality, suitable for scarves, but a heavier weight of 8 mommie is more appropriate for clothing. As a very general guide, anything under 10 mommie is considered to be a lightweight fabric; anything over is classed as a medium to heavyweight quality.

There are many different types of silk available but a lightweight silk lining material, called Habotai, is probably most widely used for silk painting. Tussah, a type of fabric produced by uncultivated silkworms, is more commonly known as 'wild silk'. Shantung is a mixture of wild and cultivated silk.

You can also obtain silk noil, twill, pongé, crêpe de chine, crêpe satin, taffeta, organza and crêpe georgette but not all of these qualities are ideal for silk painting and many of them will impose their own very different characteristics on to a design. Heavily-textured silks, for instance, will not take the paints evenly and they also intend to encourage a 'bridge' when the gutta is applied. This will later allow the watercolours to break through the resist line and run into each other.

For the inexperienced painter lightweight silk is easier to work with because resists penetrate it more rapidly and paints flow better. For your first projects keep to white silk, as this background produces clear, brilliant colours when the paints are applied. An important point to remember is that at the time of going to press, white is not represented in any range of silk paint, so the white background of the fabric is used in many designs to highlight an area, or to define outlines.

You may eventually wish to experiment with cream or pastel backgrounds. In this event, the chosen background colour will be the palest shade in a design and you will not be able to introduce any white. The background colour will also have an effect on the paints you use and it may be difficult to visualize the finished colouring of a design.

It is best to hand-wash silk before beginning to paint, to re-move any traces of dressing or grease. Wash in hand-warm water, rinse well then roll the fabric into a towel smoothing out any creases. When it is still damp, iron with a warm iron. This procedure should also be adopted when laundering a completed article.

Frames

Silk can only be painted successfully if the fabric is evenly stretched and freely suspended. If you intend to work on items of a specific size, such as scarves, it is best to use a fixed frame. If you plan to tackle projects of different sizes, such as cushions or paintings, then it will be more practical to use a frame with adjustable tension.

Before any silk is stretched on to the frame, cover the frame with adhesive tape. It can then easily be wiped clean with a damp cloth and remains of paint from previous work will not spoil a new piece of silk.

To stretch the silk over the frame, use three-point architects' thumbtacks or push pins to secure it. The three-point tacks are particularly easy to remove and will not tear the silk.

On a fixed frame, begin by pinning the four corners in place, stretching the silk and keeping it parallel to the edges of the frame. Next, secure the middle of each side, then at intervals of no more than 5 cm/2 in round all the edges. The silk needs to be stretched evenly over the frame and as tightly as a drum.

To fix the silk to an adjustable frame, set the frame to the approximate dimensions of the silk you are using. Pin the fabric to the movable bar and then on to the parallel fixed bar. Continue as given for a fixed frame, placing the pins approximately 5 cm/2 in apart while you stretch the silk. To do this, release the two screws on the movable bar and gently pull to stretch. Do not pull too hard or you may rip the fabric. When you have obtained a taut stretch, tighten the screws.

For geometric patterns or simply tracing the border of a scarf, applying gutta in a perfectly straight line can be difficult. To overcome this, take a long, straight edge such as a drawing T-shape or broomstick and place it so that the two ends rest on the frame. Supporting the ruler from underneath the fabric pinned to the frame with your free hand, trace the gutta line without changing the angle of the applicator. Avoid tracing the lines more than once, as the extra thickness will appear clumsy and mar the design.

Gutta or resist

The flow of paints is controlled by a product called 'resist' – a thick, colourless liquid sold in bottles or cans. When a thin line of resist is drawn on silk, it penetrates the fibres and stops the flow of the paints. There are two types of resist readily available; gutta, which is rubber-based, and a water-soluble resist. Both types should be shaken well before use.

The most popular way to apply gutta or resist for outlining a design is with a metal-tipped applicator bottle; water-soluble resist should only be applied by this means. A cone made of tracing paper is a suitable alternative for rubber-based gutta, but the success of this method will depend on the size of hole from which the gutta will be squeezed. When using an applicator, or a cone, it should be held like a pencil but do not slant it too much.

Making a cone: cut a rectangle 14 by 18 cm/5½ by 7 in from a piece of tracing paper. Begin by folding the paper at a 30 degree angle towards the top, then roll the paper round the triangle. Make sure that the hole at the tip is no larger than a fine needle or pin.

To close the cone, first roll a small piece of adhesive tape around the tip, making sure it does not go over the edge and block the hole. Close the remaining openings with tape, except for the top into which the gutta will be poured.

Consistency of resists: gutta is usually ready to use. It should not be too thick, which can happen when the solvent evaporates. To dilute, add a few drops of gutta solvent. Test gutta by dipping a toothpick into the liquid and holding it over a mixing cup; if the gutta forms a thin trickle, the consistency is right. Try it out on silk. Overly thick or thin gutta will not control the flow of paints. Moreover, overly thick gutta does not dry easily and will remain sticky. Water-soluble resist is ready to use and should not be diluted.

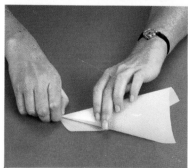

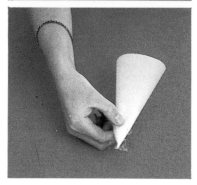

Colouring gutta: if you wish to obtain a bright colour, put a pea-sized drop of gutta colourant into a small bowl; use about quarter of that quantity for a pastel gutta. Dilute with a thimbleful of gutta solvent and add enough gutta to fill the applicator half full. Pour the mixture into the applicator or, if you are using a cone, seal it with tape.

Water-soluble resist can be discreetly coloured with only a few drops of silk paint.

Silk paints

For the projects in this book, we have used readily-available traditional silk paints. They may be diluted with a solution of 50% water and 50% ethyl rubbing alcohol, or use the special dilutant available for this purpose.

The colour charts on pages 90 and 91 show how colours of the same range can be mixed to create new colours or different tones and shades, for example, vermilion plus yellow equals orange. Colours from different ranges or from different manufacturers, however, should never be mixed. Also, it is not advisable to use gutta or fixatives of one make in combination with paints of another make.

Always test each colour on a sample strip of silk before using it directly on your project. Use white containers to mix your paints.

Quantities of paint needed: it is important to estimate ahead how much paint you will need, particularly for large even areas and when mixing colours. The heavier the silk, the more paint it will absorb. For example, to cover the background on one square metre/yard of 6 mommie silk you will need about 40 gm/2 oz of paint but for the same background on twill, you will need approximately double this quantity.

Blending paints: there are two ways of accomplishing this within an area which has been treated with resist.

1) Use paints straight out of the bottle. Place the different colours you have chosen side by side, by dipping your brush directly into one of the bottles, rinsing, then dipping it into the next, and so on. Work fast, so that the surface does not dry. If you want a lighter area, leave it white. While the surface is still wet, rinse the brush again, pick up a small amount of the water/alcohol solution and use that over the entire surface, rubbing it a little to allow the colours to blend.

2) If you are working with a large area and you are concerned about being able to paint quickly with different colours, prepare the paints in small containers instead. In some cases only a few drops will be sufficient. Apply the paints side by side, allowing them to intermix, without rinsing the brush as you go along. Avoid using too many containers and colours, so as not to become confused or have a lot of waste.

Textile paints: these paints are creamy in consistency and are set with an iron. When used without water they do not bleed on the fabric. They can be used to highlight certain details in a design.

Anti-fusant: traditional silk paints flow into each other on a fabric which has not been treated with resist outlines. An interesting new way to paint while having a certain level of control is with an anti-fusant. You can buy this produce ready to use, or prepare it yourself by mixing 20% gutta with 80% ethyl rubbing alcohol.

Shake the liquid well, spread over the entire area where you wish to avoid bleeding with a brush especially reserved for this purpose and rinsed in alcohol, then allow to dry. A thin layer is all that is needed. Pick up a small amount of paint with a separate brush and apply over the anti-fusant. The paints will not bleed. If the film applied is too thick and stops the paint from adhering, remove the excess with a brush dipped in alcohol. Use this method for fine detailed painting without resist. Use different shapes of brushes to obtain a great variety of effects.

Proceed as usual after painting with steam setting and washing. The anti-fusant will come out and the fabric will retain its free-hand painted design.

Brushes

Use a brush to apply paints to silk. Your brushes should be of good quality but not necessarily sable brushes. One fine brush and a thicker one will be sufficient for your needs. To cover large surfaces with the same colour, rather than a brush use a piece of cotton wool soaked in the required colour. Special foam brushes and foam applicators can also be used.

Painting backgrounds: once paints are applied to silk, they dry very quickly. To obtain an even background *never* go back over a dry area with a wet brush, or place wet paint next to dry paint if there is no resist to separate them. You would then have a dark edge line which is usually difficult, if not impossible to correct.

You must therefore work quickly and to cover large surfaces use foam brushes. Remember to have a fine brush handy for filling in any nooks or crannies you may have missed. See to it that the surface remains wet. Where there is a central design, paint alternatively on both sides of this, so as to keep both sides wet.

Fixing the paints

Once the painting is completed, the colours must be 'set' so that they will not run in laundering, or fade with exposure to light – this process is referred to as 'fixing'.

Prior to fixing, the painted silk is extremely fragile and must be handled carefully. It is sensitive to water, alcohol and light. Three methods of fixing can be used but follow the paint manufacturer's instructions and remember that you must never mix different types of paint and fixatives.

1) Brush-on fixative: for some ranges of paint the manufacturers recommend a fixative in liquid form. This is brushed on after the paints are dry with a broad, stiff brush – make sure all the fabric is well covered. Leave to dry for one hour or the period of time recommended by the manufacturer.

Remove the fabric from the frame and handwash in *cold water*. During this process some surplus dye may be removed, as well as any gutta used. Partly dry and when damp iron. The colours should now be permanent and set for handwashing (30°C or 86°F) and some methods of dry-cleaning.

2) Iron-setting paints: some water-based paints can be fixed by using an iron set to the temperature recommended by the manufacturer.

After the paints are dry, remove the silk from the frame, taking care that it does not touch any damp surface. Iron the silk all over the 'wrong' side. If the recommended iron temperature is too high for the fabric, protect it with a piece of plain white paper between the iron and the fabric. This method will set the colours permanently for handwashing.

3) Steam-setting paints: alcohol-based paints are best fixed by steaming in accordance with the manufacturer's instructions. The combination of heat and steam locks the colours into the fabric. Purpose-built steam ovens are available but are rather expensive. As an alternative, it is possible to use a pressure-cooker.

After the paints have dried for some hours, remove the fabric from the frame and roll it very carefully into a large piece of absorbent paper; white blotting paper or wall-paper liner are ideal. Paper with a shiny surface will not allow the steam to penetrate. The silk must be absolutely flat, with no wrinkles or creases and must not overlap or touch itself. Roll the paper and silk into a sausage-shape of about 4 cm/1½ in diameter. Close the roll with masking tape, or adhesive tape, then curve it into a wreath shape and also seal the ends.

Wrap the roll loosely in aluminium foil. The fabric must be protected in such a way that steam can reach it, but no water can come into contact with it. Partly fold the ends of the parcel to allow steam to enter but prevent condensation running into the centre of the parcel, so damaging the painted silk. Fill the pressure cooker with 2 cm/¾ in of water, or not quite to the base of the perforated basket, (see Figs a and b). Fit the foil-wrapped parcel, folded ends facing downwards, into the basket without touching the sides; place the basket on the trivet inside the pressure cooker. Moisture will condense on the lid and if drops of water fall on to the packet they may penetrate and form water spots on the fabric. To avoid this, before closing the pressure cooker, take a piece of aluminium foil, shape it into a dome and place it over the packet. Close the lid. Raise the pressure to 2.3 kg/5 lb per square 2.5 cm/1 in and steam for about 45–60 minutes. Remove the packet and allow to cool.

If a pressure cooker is not available, use a large pot with a well-fitting lid but treble the fixing time. Do not allow the pot to boil dry!

fig a shows the inside of a pressure cooker

fig b shows the level of water in the bottom of the cooker

Salt and alcohol techniques

Once the painting has been completed and *prior* to fixing the paints, marvellous mottled and spotted effects can be achieved by either applying salt to certain areas while the silk is still wet, or alcohol when the silk is dry. These techniques can also be combined in one design.

With both techniques, discretion is best. Be careful not to use too much salt and scatter it well, otherwise you may get a muddled effect. Use a small brush to apply the alcohol, pick up a small amount and then blot your brush before beginning. The alcohol spreads quickly – you can always add more but you cannot take away!

Humidity plays a role in these techniques. With the salt, be sure it is completely dry for maximum effect and that the fabric is wet. With the alcohol, the fabric must be completely dry to produce a mottled effect.

Salt technique: this consists of scattering various kinds of salt over a wet surface. You can use coarse salt, table salt or salt crystals. Each grain of salt will attract the paint towards it by absorbing the water. The result is a lovely spotted effect which is completely unpredictable.

Alcohol technique: this is obtained by placing a brush dipped in alcohol on to a dry painted surface. The alcohol repulses the colour and thereby produces light coloured spots, surrounded by an outline of concentrated colour.

Above: applying salt to a wet fabric.
Below: applying alcohol to a dry fabric.

Colouring

All the designs given in this book have been painted with traditional colours, which can be diluted with water and alcohol. These colours can be mixed together in endless combinations, therefore you do not need to buy a lot of different paints. From just a few primary colours you can produce all the tones you need and use them pure, or diluted in varying strengths.

1) red + yellow

2) yellow + blue

3) red + brown

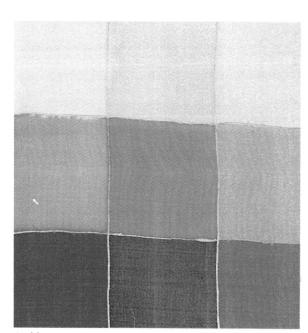

4) blue + green

In the squares numbered one to six we have mixed two colours together, then lightened the tones obtained. In the vertical bands numbered seven to nine, one colour has been mixed with two or three others in succession.

These last three examples are just suggestions. If you test all the possible combinations yourself you will gradually become aware of the subtleties of different mixtures. The best way is to test them on a little piece of silk.

As you progress in expertise you will find you may need more than just one of the primary colours, red, yellow, blue and black. You won't, for example, be able to obtain a true violet from, say, vermilion red and blue but will need a bright scarlet. Every brand of paint contains a set of basic colours from which you can obtain all the others, so ask your supplier for his advice.

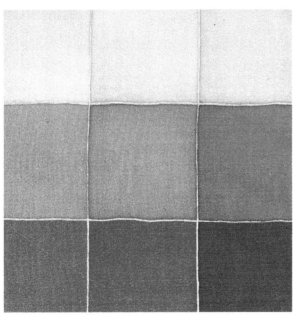

5) pink + blue

6) black + yellow

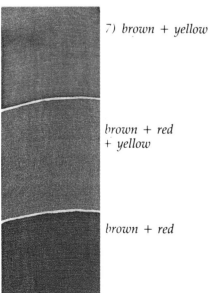

7) brown + yellow

brown + red + yellow

brown + red

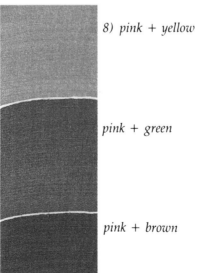

8) pink + yellow

pink + green

pink + brown

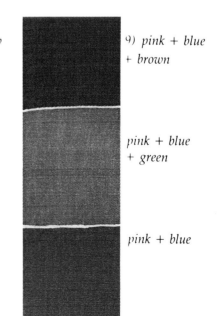

9) pink + blue + brown

pink + blue + green

pink + blue

How to enlarge or reduce a design

The previous pages in this book give diagrams of designs and motifs which you can copy. To enable them to fit into the page size they have been considerably reduced and to produce the size indicated in the instructions, the design must be traced out to the measurements given on the squared grid. As an example, if the measurement for one square of a grid is given as 3 cm/1¼ in and the design covers ten squares, the finished size of the painting will be 30 cm/11¾ in, (see Figs a and b).

You may, of course, wish to enlarge the actual drawing beyond the size we have given, or even reduce it, and there are several ways which will enable you to obtain an exact copy. Various forms of photocopiers will enlarge or reduce a diagram on paper and more sophisticated machines will copy a design to any size, on any material, but these are rather costly.

The simplest way to enlarge or reduce a drawing, however, is to use a pantograph, which you can either make yourself, or obtain from most art or craft shops, (see Fig c). A pantograph consists of four flattened rods, or pieces of wood. At the appropriate points, a tracing point is fixed to these rods for tracing over the lines of the original, and a drawing point for making the copy. The pantograph is hinged at the crossing points and can be adjusted to enlarge or reduce the copy.

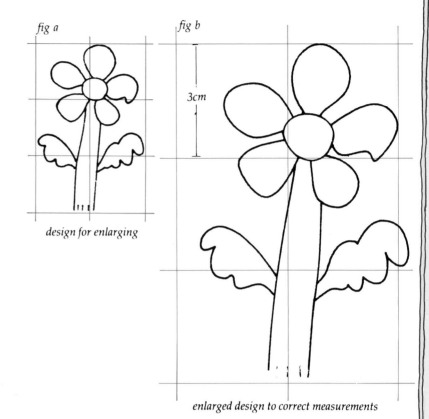

fig a

fig b

3cm

design for enlarging

enlarged design to correct measurements

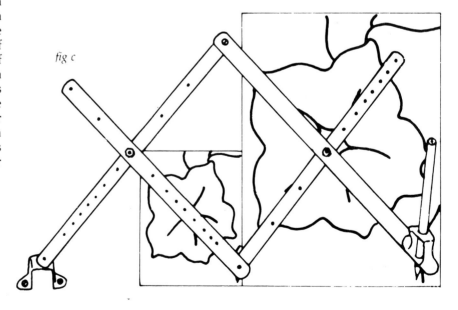

fig c

drawing of a pantograph

How to transfer designs on to silk

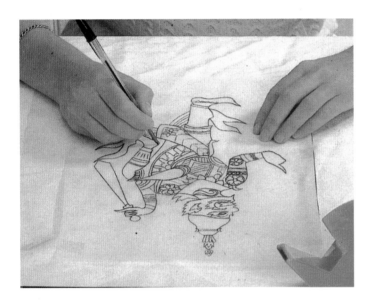

Once you have produced a drawing to the correct size needed for the design you have in mind, there are two ways of transferring it on to the silk.

1) Place tracing paper over the drawing and trace over the outlines with a heavy, waterproof marker. With the silk stretched tightly over the frame, place the traced design *under* the silk and hold it lightly in position with adhesive tape at the corners. Outline the design directly with resist, then remove the taped tracing and proceed to paint.

2) For greater precision, trace the design with a pencil on the wrong side of the tracing paper. Place the tracing paper wrong side down over the silk, which is placed flat on a table, and go over all the outlines again. The pencil lines will show lightly on the silk and when the silk is stretched over the frame, you will be able to outline the design with resist.

Problems with gutta and corrections

TYPE OF PROBLEM	REASONS	CORRECTIONS
The lines of gutta are too wide and uneven, with a 'blob' at the beginning and the end. Poor control.	– The gutta is flowing too fast because the opening is too wide.	– Make a new paper cone with a smaller hole. – Place a small piece of paper at the start and the end of a line to catch the 'blob' or starting drop This is especially useful when using an applicator.
Spots of gutta.	– The silk is not tautly stretched and touches the work surface; the lines spread and smear. – The cone is not tightly closed or you are squeezing too hard which allows the gutta to escape. – The applicator is not tightly closed.	– Stretch the silk again. – Make a new cone or seal the cracks with tape. – The gutta does not come out of the cone or applicator because it is too thick. Add some gutta solvent and place into a fresh cone. If the hole is too small; enlarge it with a needle. – You have placed too much gutta in the cone. Empty it and fill again.
The gutta does not work effectively, paints breach the dam and jump the line of resist.	– The gutta is too thick. – The gutta did not completely penetrate the fabric. – The gutta is too liquid. – The gutta is of poor quality.	– Prepare another cone and add more solvent to the gutta. – Add more solvent to the gutta and use a new cone. On heavier fabrics it might also be necessary to apply the gutta on the reverse side. – Open the cone, allow the solvent to evaporate from the gutta and use a new cone.
The gutta has breaks in the line and paints run through the openings.	– You have left openings, however tiny, in the lines. – The applicator skipped on the silk while you were applying the gutta and has created an uneven line.	– Be sure you have good lighting where you work and go over the openings again before you proceed to paint. – The tape may have gone beyond the tip of the cone, make another cone. – You have been pushing too hard on the silk, use a lighter touch. – You are working against the grain of the silk. Try to move with the fibres.

Problems with paints and corrections

TYPE OF PROBLEM	REASONS	CORRECTIONS
Background colours are uneven and they streak or have dark edge areas.	– You have diluted your paints too much and they are unstable. – Your brush was not clean. – There is too much water and not enough alcohol in your mixed paint.	– Try a special fluid for diluting paint which slows down the drying process and helps to avoid streaking. – Clean all your tools very well. – Modify your mixed paint by using different proportions of water + alcohol.
Backgrounds are uneven, the colours show dark edge lines and light spots.	– You went back over a dry area. – You applied fresh paint next to dry paint.	– The fabric should always remain wet while you are working.
Spot of colour on a white surface.	– Clumsiness. – Gap in the gutta line.	– Check the gutta and close the opening in the line if necessary. – Clean the spot with a cotton swab dipped in alcohol while you place a cotton ball underneath.
Spot on an area which has already been painted.	– Clumsiness. – Gap in the gutta line.	– If the spot is located within a small area, moisten the entire area again with a brush dipped in alcohol and rub where the spot is. Remove as much paint as possible from the edges with a drier brush. Repeat this operation several times then apply paint again. – If the spot is on a large surface, there is not much you can do about it. In general you can save a background with a problem by: 1. Moistening the entire area and scattering coarse salt. 2. Using alcohol to add spots thus masking the problem.

Index

If readers have difficulty obtaining any of the materials or equipment mentioned in this book, please write for further information to the publishers.
Search Press Ltd , Wellwood, North Farm Road, Tunbridge Wells, Kent TN2 3DR, England

If you are interested in any other of the art and craft titles published by Search Press please send for free colour catalogue to:
Search Press Ltd, Dept B, Wellwood, North Farm Road, Tunbridge Wells, Kent TN2 3DR, England